DELYS SARGEANT, AM, was previously head of the Social Biology Resources Centre at the University of Melbourne and during the 1980s a weekly commentator on 'life and relationships' on national radio. Now she is president of the Council on the Ageing, Victoria, vice-president of COTA nationally, and an adviser to several governments and agencies concerned with older Australians, women's health, public health and similar concerns.

ANNE UNKENSTEIN is a clinical neuropsychologist specialising in memory loss, consulting at the Memory Clinic, North West Hospital, Parkville, Melbourne, and in private practice. She is also an academic associate of the School of Behavioural Sciences, Department of Psychology at the University of Melbourne, a community educator and regular guest speaker for the Council on the Ageing.

To Mick, Madeleine, William and 'Playschool'   A.U.

To John, Adele and Michael; and to the friends and colleagues who
contributed so much to my memories, many of whose names
I've forgotten!   D.S.

HOW MEMORY WORKS

AND WHAT TO DO

WHEN IT DOESN'T

remembering well

Delys Sargeant & Anne Unkenstein

ALLEN & UNWIN

First published in 1998 by
Allen & Unwin Pty Ltd
9 Atchison St, St Leonards, NSW 2065 Australia
Phone: (61 2) 9901 4088
Fax: (61 2) 9906 2218
E-mail: frontdesk@allen-unwin.com.au
URL: http://www.allen-unwin.com.au

10 9 8 7 6 5 4 3 2 1

National Library of Australia
cataloguing-in-publication entry:

Sargeant, Delys.
Remembering well: how memory works, and what to do when it doesn't.

 Bibliography.
 Includes index.
 ISBN 1 86448 358 X.

 1. Memory. 2. Memory – Age factors. 3. Memory disorders.
 I. Unkenstein, Anne E. II. Title.

153.12

Cover photos used courtesy of Rob Goldman/FPG/Austral (hands),
Joe McBride/Tony Stone (eye) and Ruth Grüner
Cover design by Ruth Grüner
Text designed by Kim Roberts
Typeset by J&M Typesetting
Printed in Australia by Australian Print Group, Maryborough, Victoria

Acknowledgements

We sincerely thank friends, colleagues and family who showed commitment in time and attention to detail: David Ames, Elvala Ayton, Stephen Bowden, Sarah Brenan, Lyn Hattam, Julie and Wallace Meehan, Mary and Fred Symons, Helen and Ian Unkenstein, Jackie Yowell, and the Council on the Ageing (Victoria). We are also grateful to Mandy Gill of Age Concern New Zealand, and Anne Studner of the American Association of Retired Persons.

*Some of the proceeds from this book will
promote positive ageing by contributing to the
Council on the Ageing (COTA).*

Contents

Introduction

'My memory's hopeless these days...' How often have we said that, or heard someone else say it? Sometimes there's a note of anxiety, and no wonder. After all, memory is an essential part of one's identity; it makes meaning of the past and brings order to the bustle of everyday experience. We are not ourselves without it.

We wrote this book because we both are involved with people who declare a concern about their memories not working well for them, and because we are intrigued at the experience of memory changes as people age. For Delys as an over-65-year-old involved in health promotion, there was a personal interest as well as the professional one she shares with Anne, who is in her early thirties and works in a memory clinic as a neuropsychologist.

People asked us, 'Where do you go if you have concerns about remembering? What memory changes are normal as you get older? Could it be the beginnings of Alzheimer's Disease? What can we do to manage change in memory abilities? Should I turn to one of the "memory improvement" courses now available?' These are the sorts of questions we set out to answer.

Delys went through the experience described several times in this book, of feeling that she was 'losing' her memory abilities and wondering if this might be the beginnings of dementia. Having consulted

Anne and done some memory tests, she was reassured; but she was interested in other people's reactions to her seeking the assessment. It became evident that the subject of memory loss was of keen interest, especially but not exclusively to older people—the biggest turn-up ever for an annual general meeting of the Council on the Ageing, Victoria was one at which Anne was advertised as guest speaker on the topic of memory—and that all sorts of powerful taboos surrounded it. Paradoxically, although people seem hungry for information about how to remember well, there seems to be an equal desire not to find out if their memory really is failing ('I'm really OK', 'I wouldn't want to know', 'Nothing can be done about it' are common attitudes). Memory testing has long been available, yet it is an area of health care many people don't use.

We found that children at school, adolescents learning new ideas and skills, young adults in new relationships through to the venerable old, all have anxieties, often poorly expressed, that they will experience change in their memory abilities; but the people who typically express most concern are adults from their late thirties on. Women particularly showed an interest in reading this book, and many of them quickly added, 'And I'll give it to my mother too!' This reaction was common across cultures: women from Wales, Singapore, China, the Philippines, Vietnam, Canada, New Zealand and different parts of Australia all said the same. Men also nominated their mothers as likely to benefit, but few of them saw it as being relevant to their own lives, and fathers were less often identified as likely to be in need by either sons or daughters.

Clearly, the issue of gender and memory warrants further study!

What people are most concerned about, in our experience, is memory change over which they have no control; a sense that they are losing mental capacities they once had. We do not explore in this book the various forms of therapeutic work with long-term memories. We are concerned primarily with the everyday remembering that is such an important part of our lives in society. Schoolchildren have to remember names, places, timetables, words of songs, formulae, even if they no longer have to learn mathematical tables or poetry off by heart. In the world of work we rely on our memory of telephone numbers, names of contacts, account numbers and passwords. At leisure we may need to remember cards at bridge, be quick at TV and radio quiz shows, recall words for crossword puzzles, or names of old films or pieces of music, or where we left the car keys! We remember technical procedures like how to drive a car, fix a fuse or set up a spreadsheet on the PC. At home we need to know addresses, birthday dates and anniversaries. The list goes on. Every hour of the day we're calling on memory. Our capacity to respond to these demands depends on our state of mind at the time, on our health and to some extent on our age.

We believe it is important to acknowledge that for many people as they go through life, memory abilities do change in some ways. The changes that occur are usually very mild, and some people do not even notice them. However, for those people who do notice the changes—either in themselves, or in a friend or relative, a 'nearest and dearest'—it helps to be open to discussion about 'reasonable' or expected or 'normal' changes in our mental processing, and about ways of adapting to them. The good news is that we can become more skilful in managing our memory; we have more memories to integrate, play and be creative with; and we have more opportunities to use the present in relation to the past and the future—and perhaps, grow in wisdom. The wise use of memory-enhancing strategies is one of the aims we hold for readers of this book.

Our aim is to present the facts about memory change and give practical guidance for remembering well for people of all ages, using real-life stories for illustration. We suggest places you might go for help—but remember that health infrastructures vary from place to place, and generalisations about memory clinics, or the role of doctor and neuropsychologist, for example, need to be checked. We also introduce the concept of a 'memory-friendly society' in which the community positively acknowledges and supports memory change in adults.

Memory change is a reality over the whole of our lives. This book explains how memory works and what to do when it doesn't. Use it as a starting point to make remembering well part of your life!

How memory works

It is tempting to make all-or-none statements about memory as if it were a single concept. You might say 'My memory is letting me down', for example—but is it a problem with remembering what you did yesterday, or what you did when you were a child? If a person is said to have a 'fantastic memory', is it for remembering names, or for recalling trivia? When we register a familiar aroma—lavender, Johnson's Baby Powder, eucalypt, burning pine cones, Dad's shed—and it triggers a burst of feelings and memories that we thought we had forgotten, is the same process at work as when we recall facts and figures? What about community memory, represented in things like commemorative stamps, statues and symbols, in oral history, and in language itself?

Memory is, in fact, a very complex phenomenon: a whole book could be written outlining the current theories and debate about how memory works and its neurophysiological basis. (It is also mediated by culture: in some societies much more value is assigned to, say, musical memory skills, visualisation or the ability to remember complex dance movements than in others.) We don't want to get too technical here, but a simple model of memory may be useful to understand which parts of the 'works' could need special care and attention.

The starting point is to think of memory as a storage system. Storage facilities are all around us—the refrigerator, the pantry, wardrobes, photo albums, computers, even department stores. Of course, some systems are more streamlined than others—locating a particular item in a library is usually much easier than finding the thing you want in your junk room!—but the procedures for using them are the same. Think of the good old filing cabinet; you put your selected work-related documents, family budgeting information or recipes into labelled folders, you store them in the cabinet, and you get them out when you want them. In other words, you **acquire** and deposit information, you **store** information and you **recall** information.

In principle, these same processes are also a part of memory.

Getting things you want to remember into the files (acquiring)

Immediate memory

So we have our filing cabinet ready to be filled up with more new memories. How do we get them in there? There are a few steps in this process.

First we **pay attention** to the information—we need to be awake and alert here—and it goes into a small temporary store, often referred to as immediate memory. You could think of **immediate memory** as your in-tray, which you keep on top of your filing cabinet. Later the information goes into more enduring storage.

This is how your immediate memory works:

- You **do not process** or manipulate the information that goes into it. The information gets in and sits in your in-tray without being checked over or organised in any way.
- It can only hold a small amount of information at one time. Your in-tray is small and has a very **limited capacity**. It holds from five to nine items at one time.
- The next information that you put into this temporary store will wipe out what was in it before. Each time new items are placed in your in-tray, the previous items are moved out to make more room.

Now, have a go at using your immediate memory so that you can test out what we're talking about.

Read the following telephone number slowly. When you have finished reading it, stop, and say the telephone number to yourself: 9412 1956.

Now, here's some more information to put into your in-tray.

You are at a meeting and someone introduces herself to you. She says, 'Hello, I'm Rita Sullivan.' Now repeat the name to yourself.

After you put the name 'Rita Sullivan' into your in-tray, you probably found it hard to remember the phone number that you've just repeated. If so, it was moved out, to make more room. This type of memory is good for remembering a phone number long enough to dial it, but doesn't last long enough for you to dial the same number again half an hour later (or even five minutes later!).

Enduring memory

Let's say that you want to save that phone number for later use, but you don't have a pen and paper handy to write it down. Or perhaps you want to remember Rita Sullivan's name, because you are likely to meet her again. To remember these bits of information later, you will have to move them from your in-tray into more durable storage, inside your filing cabinet.

To do this you will have to **process or manipulate it in some way**. These manipulations can happen without your being aware of it, but more often you do it intentionally. For example, you might repeat a number a few times or divide it into two or more sections to be remembered separately; you might repeat a name a few times, concentrate on its spelling or think how it is similar to the name of a person that you know very well. People sometimes use quite complex reminders which have personal significance.

I will always remember the phone number for our local take-away pizza shop. The first digits are the local dialling code, and the last four digits are 1956, the year that the Olympics were in my home town – Melbourne!   Jane

When it is a name which is likely to be very important for me to recall accurately, I consciously change the way I am standing or sitting when I hear

the name, repeat the name after I have left the person and as soon as
possible find a pen and paper to record it.   **Delys**

At other times, people acquire or collect new memories without realising it until they recall them later. This could happen when you are
looking for your keys, for example. When you put the keys down,
you didn't try to remember where you put them. However, when it
comes to finding them later, most times you will remember without
too much active recalling where you put them.

Whether new information gets in intentionally or not, it still goes
through the same basic processing. It's just that sometimes you don't
realise the process is occurring. You pay attention to something, it
goes into your immediate memory in-tray, and from there, it is
processed for the more durable storage files within your memory
filing cabinet.

Scientists think that information can be more difficult to get out of
a memory file later on if it has not been processed in a meaningful and
well-organised way. For instance, if you shove something into your
filing cabinet in a rushed way, without paying attention to the information and thinking about which file it should be put in, it can be difficult to find again later. If, on the other hand, you classify it, label it,
and put it into a mental folder that contains other similar files, it
should be much easier to locate later on.

There are many different 'filing tabs' that we use in our filing cabinet—files can be organised by what they look, sound, smell, taste or
feel like. We might group files according to context—family, work,
hobbies and so on. This idea is important when we think of **memory
strategies,** a topic that we will return to in Chapter 5.

⚙ Having a good safe filing cabinet (storing)

This **more enduring storage** that we've been talking about is your true filing cabinet. It's where all kinds and any amounts of memories can be stored. Some are very emotional, some sad, some happy. You will store things that you've heard, seen, smelled, tasted or touched. Things in here can be very organised or a complete mess of disorganised data (like a badly organised fridge!).

You can put as much information as you like into these files—there is no known limit to the amount of information that can go into storage. Your filing cabinet is bottomless. You can store information here for very long periods of time—sometimes for over 90 years!

Recent memory storage

Recent memories are those from this morning, yesterday and last week. What did you have for dinner last night? What happened in the TV serial last Sunday? What was that telephone message earlier today?

Recent memories are the ones that many of us complain about forgetting.

Lifetime memory storage

What we hold in lifetime memory storage, and the way we organise it, is different for each person.

You can store:

• **Personal memories** from your own life history that contribute to your beliefs, your behaviours.

• Information about your **area of expertise** at work or at home. You might remember and know a lot about fishing, accounting, gardening or building.

- Memories of **familiar places**, such as special landscapes, towns, parks, supermarkets—and the way to get around them.
- Memories of **procedures**, or knowledge of how to do things. Your store of procedures will include the activities that you have learned well and have practised regularly during your life, like driving, knitting, typing, making a sauce, etc.
- **General knowledge** information that comes in very handy for games such as trivial pursuit and quiz shows, and answering questions from your grandchildren!
- You also store **conceptual knowledge and general rules**, that you have accumulated over time; for example, arithmetical concepts (addition, subtraction, etc.) or different shapes (round, square, etc.), or knowledge that the earth is round and you won't fall off it because of gravity!

> What are some of the lifetime memories that are occupying many files in your filing cabinet? What are in some of your special skills files, your areas of expertise files? What files do you have of procedures that have become so automatic you do not have to actively think about the steps involved?

 ## Getting things out when you need to use them (recalling)

There comes a time when you want to get memories out again, and sometimes quickly! This process is often called 'recall'. Sometimes recall is for exact detail—for example, 'What is the French word for clock?', or 'What is her name?'. But even when we remember a number, a sentence, a poem by rote, we 'flavour' it with a meaning which is special for us as individuals. Some may remember a classroom scene when they recall a poem of Wordsworth, or who they were once with as they say a prayer, or the smell of an injury when dialling an emergency telephone number or when repeating a nursery rhyme to a little child there are vivid recollections of earlier learnings of the rhyme.

What we recall from our memory files is usually quite selective, and it is not always a replica or mirror image of what went in—it is reconstructed or reassembled. Even the most accurate recall will not be as exact a 'copy' as if we were pulling out the original document or the original sound or smell which was filed in our memory storage. We re-interpret, build up again or even redesign the information in the smallest or the grandest way when we bring the 'stuff' we want to remember up out of storage.

'But how can you say that was what Dad told us—I was there at the time and I didn't hear him say it like that!' Robert to Susan

Our beliefs, our values, our perceptions not only affect what we select to put into storage—they also influence what we actually choose to remember and if Susan wants to influence her recollections because of how she values Robert, she will challenge her own memory and maybe reconstruct her perception of how her mother spoke.

Memory is a net; one finds it full of fish when he takes it from the brook; but a dozen miles of water have run through it without sticking.
Oliver W. Holmes Sr, 1858

Recall processes

Sometimes your filing cabinet falls open automatically and presents you with an 'uncalled-for' memory. This often happens because of **association,** and associations are often triggered by smell.

I was amazed to suddenly recall an event, out of the blue it seemed, when I must have been about eight years of age: my father was watching me drive the Caterpillar tractor, for the very first time on my own around the yard. I could see him with the pigpen yards behind him and even smell the pigs! He was coming over to the tractor. I could see the control panel very clearly. Then I heard him saying loudly, 'Pull that lever down, John'. It was SO CLEAR—what brought this into my mind just then? I know, I was driving past a farm and the smell of pigs was so strong!   John, 60

Smell can be overwhelmingly nostalgic because it triggers powerful images and emotions before we have time to edit them...

When we give perfume to someone, we give them liquid memory. Kipling was right: 'Smells are surer than sights and sounds to make your heart strings crack.'[1]

Memories can also be associated with particular times of the year.

Each Christmas when I open the Christmas tree decorations box, memories come flooding back to me of past Christmas times. Each decoration has a story that goes with it, especially the hand-made ones.   Elizabeth

I well remember so much about Christmas days when we were young competing with my brothers in how many threepences were in the Christmas pudding, opening the Christmas stocking before anyone else was awake, helping to cook the Christmas dinner in the heat of a Western Australian summer day, preparing the Christmas tree and opening the box of decorations from so many years before!   Delys

I have my saddest times when I remember some of the events which occurred around Christmas Day—of arguments over who should prepare certain foods, of unwelcome family announcements, of people who have died and aren't with us any more, of people who have preferred to share Christmas with others...I am starting to dread the 25th of December.   **Mary**

Unprompted memories can also occur by recognition. You may be watching a film, and realise that you've seen it before. You might not remember someone's name when you see them at a wedding, but you may recognise it when you see it on the list of names for the seating arrangement. You see the photo of a landscape and remember an event of your childhood or a holiday.

Intentional or free recall

Free recall occurs when you want to remember something, and go searching through your memory storage files to find it—the author of the book you are reading, the joke your friend told you last week, the name of the wine you had last night, the time you are to be picked up.

The ability to fantasise, which contributes to the life quality of many people, is dependent on the ability to free recall from memory storage.

To be able to enjoy one's past life is to live twice. Martial, Epigrams (AD 86)

Have a go at some free recall from your past, or generate a wonderful fantasy!

Think back to an experience from your school days—for example, winning a prize, making a special friend, the sound of a particular teacher or losing your best pen. Remember it in as much detail as possible. For example, what was the name of the school? How old were you? Who else was there? Where

were you sitting or standing? What year it did it happen in? Perhaps you can
even remember the school motto or song?

Thinking about this experience entails recall of information that was
put in your lifetime memory storage a long time ago. You may find
some details easier to recall than others, and if the recall is repeated
some hours later, more details may emerge.

We often try to promote free recall when we use **intention to
remember**. How often do we say 'I must remember to remember
that' or 'I mustn't forget that'. Later on, we have to recall what it was
that we told ourselves to remember. It might be to video-record a
show on TV, or to remember the title of a film that a friend recommended. But it can be very frustrating at times! You might have a
word on the tip of your tongue, but no matter how hard you try, you
can't recall it. What was her name? What is the word for the entree
that you have before an Italian meal?

When we learn something new, we usually draw on free recall. Use
free recall to remember this new very important information!

What is the title of this book?
What is in the picture on the front cover?
What is distinctive about using this book?

Recall can be made easier if we use other information or a special cue
to trigger the memory. This is called **cued recall**.

What sort of cues do you use to trigger memories? Have you ever cued your
memory to help find something you have mislaid?

If you couldn't find your wallet, the cue that you might use would be
to think 'Where did I have my wallet last?'. If you meet up with a
man in the street, but can't remember his name, you can sometimes

cue your memory by thinking about the context that you usually see him in. Is he someone from the sports club, from work or from your street? For many people, photos are specially important visual cues for past memories.

If I came home and saw my house on fire the first thing I would try to get out would be my photo negatives. My photos are my personal history. I'd hate to be without them.   **Len**

We will return to the idea of cued recall in more detail when we discuss memory strategies in Chapter 5.

There are times when we recall information from storage without realising it. For example, many of the steps involved in playing the piano, knitting, riding a bicycle, driving a car, cooking roast dinner or rice, or setting the table are procedures which have become automatic.

I'm home with my first baby, and constantly feel that I'm on a 'steep learning curve' when it comes to being a parent. I often catch myself saying 'How do you know how to do that, Mum?'. 'I don't know really—I've just always done it that way,' she replies. Everything seems so easy for her, in comparison to my fumbling fingers. She seems to fold the nappies without thinking, and makes baby bathing look so easy.   **Monica**

We are constantly using different memory processes. Our memory filing cabinet is almost never shut. Sometimes remembering works well for us, at other times we notice lapses. Memory is dynamic. There are constant fluctuations in all of our memory processes—in getting information in, storing it and getting what we want out.

In the next two chapters we will explore some of the factors that can enhance the dynamics of our memory across the years of our life.

Key points

- Memory is not a single 'thing'. At the simplest level, it involves:

  acquiring—paying attention, putting into immediate memory and more enduring memory;

  storing—according to when stored and type of memory (event, concept, procedure);

  recalling—by association, recognition, free and cued recall.

- Memories are selective and are reconstructed; they are not exact replicas of experience.

- Memory is dynamic, and influenced by many factors.

2

How memory changes as we get older

Mummy, it is my forgettery that worries me, not my memory!

Jane, 5

I know I'll remember—don't hassle me—give me some time to think! Where are my keys? Has anyone seen them? I know I put them in the usual place...Yes, I do have a usual place: it's right by the phone—I'm in a rush, can someone please help me find them? (Well, I'm not the only one who loses things: stop telling me what I should have done and help me look for them.) I know I leave things to the last minute—don't keep telling me off, help me! Here they are—I should have remembered deciding this was the best place to leave them. (What is wrong with me that I didn't remember where I had left those keys? I can't discuss this with Joe—he'll only tell me off again for 'not being responsible' and then he'll get angry again about me keeping on forgetting, and I will get angry that he can't listen to my fear about being forgetful. Maybe I should have a whole lot of keys cut, give him one and then stash them all around the place?   Jenny

As we get older, the most common change that we complain about is memory change. People have problems remembering names, dates of appointments coming up or where they've put something; sometimes they describe going into a room and thinking 'What did I come in here to get?'.

If we experience these problems as a younger person, we tend to blame them on lack of effort or lack of attention. As we get older, and experience the same memory lapses, we begin to wonder about our actual memory ability, and blame our age.

Many of us have a pessimistic outlook about getting older. Fear of 'senility' which is often seen as an inevitable consequence of ageing lingers on in the general literature, in birthday cards (go and look in your local newsagency), advertisements, and in conversations. The fact is that our main sources of information—the media—continue to focus on abnormal and negative aspects of ageing and this has a powerful influence on society attitudes. We are regularly exposed to portrayals of public figures experiencing memory loss and dementia (one popular television series, for example, portrayed a forgetful, manipulative old woman who continued to harass and scapegoat her hapless son).

Researchers have given medical names to the everyday memory problems that are often experienced as people get older. 'Benign Senescent Forgetfulness' (introduced in 1962) was compared to more incapacitating kinds of memory change, such as the dementias. 'Age

Associated Memory Impairment' came up in 1986. More recently, in 1992, this term was replaced by 'Age Associated Cognitive Decline', to encompass changes that happen with normal ageing to other mental abilities apart from memory. (How would you like to be described as an 'Age Associated Cognitive Decliner'?!) At one stage, there was even a push to include terms such as these in the manual commonly used in medical practice in the diagnosis of psychiatric disorders.[2]

What names do you hear people using to describe themselves? Perhaps 'vague' or 'forgetful' have less stigma than some of the medical names listed above!

The current outlook on memory and ageing

In the previous chapter, different memory processes were outlined. Only some of these change as people get older. Many are found not to be affected at all, and some can improve, so the picture is certainly not one of dramatic, inevitable and accelerating decline.

For many people, changes in particular memory processes happen so gradually that they are not thought of as a problem. For others, the changes are only obvious in situations where they are required to push their memory abilities to the limit.

The bulk of past memory research involved stretching people's memory abilities to the utmost, and has resulted in an unnecessarily pessimistic view of the effect of old age on memory abilities. Typical research involved comparing the performance of young and old people on the same memory tests. Older people may have performed worse on testing, not because of their age, but due to comparative differences in their health or level of education. Younger people could have been advantaged by familiarity with the type of tests used and the environment in which they were conducted. Moreover, many of the tests used measured speed of response, rather then actual memory ability. (It is well known that younger people process information more rapidly than older people. They get new information into their storage files faster. We have all had the experience of observing how quickly five-year-olds learn how to use new technology!) Finally, we should not forget that motivated older people can use life skills and adapt their learning by being very strategic (see Chapter 5), using their developed wisdom to manage effective learning.

Memory abilities at any age will be different for one person compared to another. One person may have an extraordinary talent for remembering the number plates of friends' cars. Another person will embarrass you by always remembering to send birthday cards on time, when you always forget! (Little do you know—they have a well organised reminder system—a birthday book.) More and more variation is seen between people's abilities as they get older.

There are many factors that have been found to enhance this variability between people of the same age, and even in the same individual from day to day. These will be discussed in Chapter 3.

Which memory processes change as we get older?

Recent research has described the effect of getting older on **attention** processes, the ability to **get new information into storage**, the **time that it takes** to recall things, and the '**tip of the tongue**' experience. It is often a combination of these changes, with other health, lifestyle and attitudinal factors, that sometimes makes our memory more unreliable as we get older.

Attention

Research has shown that as we get older we can experience change in our ability to pay attention, and our ability to ignore distractions. This can be made worse by mild hearing loss.

It has been shown that older people cannot focus attention on as much information at the same time as younger people. Furthermore, older people can find it difficult to shift their attention back and forth between two tasks. This may mean that it is harder to follow two conversations at the same time, or it may be more difficult to do several things at the same time. For instance, reading a book with music playing in the background and at the same time remembering to not let the casserole in the oven overcook, or driving someone else's car with the radio on.

Older people have also been shown to have more difficulty resisting distraction. Distraction can be internal or external. A common internal distraction is when we are thinking about something else or registering pain and find that we have let our mind wander. A common external distraction is the telephone. You are busy doing something when the telephone rings. You answer the phone, and later find it hard to remember what you were doing before the telephone interrupted you.

In these situations we have trouble getting new information into our storage files, because we are finding it harder to pay attention to it.

The ability to remember new things

As we have discussed in the previous chapter, remembering something new involves the processes of acquiring and recalling. Recent research has shown that these two processes are the most affected as we get older.

As we age we have more difficulty on tests that involve remembering things that we have just seen or heard. Older people have been found to be less likely than younger people to use memory strategies, such as the way they organise their thinking, what they associate with information, or how they 'see' things in their mind, to help them to acquire or recall new information. The information may be stored, but unless it is well filed, it is hard to get at when needed. When you put a library book back on the wrong shelf, or the balsamic vinegar bottle in with the wine bottles, it is as good as missing.

Researchers have begun to ask why is it that many older people don't spontaneously make use of strategies to help them remember new things. Could it be that older people were never taught to use these strategies? Many older people of today were taught to rely on rote learning, while school education has more recently focused on using meaning and association to remember.

Or could it be that using such strategies is more difficult for older people because they are slower to process information? Information is often presented rapidly, and older people may need more time than when they were younger to organise it into the proper files in their filing system.

The time that it takes to remember things

Mastering something new takes more time as we age. Extra time may be required for practice and review in order to acquire new skills, such as speaking a new language or managing the intricacies of the computer and the Internet!

It can take longer to get information out of the storage files, as well as into them, when we get older. This is most evident when an immediate response to something is required. You might suddenly have to recall someone's name when you meet them in the street, or you might be asked to respond quickly to a request for a changed date for a dinner engagement.

The impact of this slowing is not so obvious in responding to familiar or more routine requests for quick memory recall. If an activity is second nature it can be performed without a great deal of mental effort and the 'normal' slowing associated with older age doesn't affect it so much.

The 'tip of the tongue' experience

'Memory is often not so much lost as hard to find.' Steven Rose[3]

Most of us have had the 'tip of the tongue' experience. We say, 'What is that word…I know it, but I can't recall it', or 'What is that person's name—I know it so well, but it won't come to me'. Whenever we want to remember something, we review the contents of the files in our filing cabinet. People of all ages can experience 'blocking'—when a search for particular information is not successful.

'I know it's there, but it won't come up!'

A 'tip of the tongue' experience occurs when our search process gets close to the word or name, but we cannot 'locate' the file for it. This is different to recalling something that we have just learned. It involves sorting through old storage files for a memory that has been there for a long time, and that we know very well is in there for us to find.

Research has shown that we experience the 'tip of the tongue' problem more often as we get older. Some researchers suggest that this is because our storage files get larger as we get older and we have more information to search through. Names of people are a common example. Perhaps, after a lifetime of meeting people it becomes more difficult to pluck out one particular name, especially if it is similar to many other names that we have stored in our files.

Another theory relates to the context that we are in when we are doing a memory search of our files. It is much easier to identify and name someone when we always see them in the same place or at predictable times. But we all know how difficult it can be to remember someone's name when we meet up with them unexpectedly in a new context. As we get older, it seems, we become more dependent on contextual cues.

So: as we get older our rememberings are influenced by our ability to attend, the context (the where and when), needing more time to process our files, and the fact that we have more stuff stored in our files (some of which we may not have organised very well!).

Which areas of memory will *not* be affected by age?

Recent research suggests that the memory processes that do not change as we get older are immediate memory and lifetime memory. They don't involve a time limit, and/or tend to occur almost automatically, and/or don't require the use of strategies, and, in the case of lifetime memories, benefit from using accumulated experience.

Immediate memory

We talked about immediate memory in the last chapter. Immediate memory is a temporary store which has a limited capacity (our 'in-tray'). Information goes into this store before it is processed for more enduring memory storage. Getting older does not generally affect immediate memory. **As long as you are not distracted**, a test of ability is for you to recall five to nine words or numbers immediately after you hear or see them. Most older people retain such ability, as long as they are able to pay attention.

Lifetime memory

We listed the various forms of lifetime memory in the previous chapter: personal memories; information about your area of expertise at work or at home; memories of familiar places; memories of procedures; general knowledge and conceptual knowledge. Such memories are very enduring. They also keep accumulating. Many older people seek to widen their knowledge by reading, listening to the radio, watching television or enrolling in education programmes.

Older persons who spend a lot of time recalling past life experiences can be negatively judged by family and friends as 'living in the past', or 'boring'. Yet some people use such reminiscences to work on 'unfinished business', which may often be very emotive or painful. Alternatively, the stories may be highly valued as contributions to family and community memory. In some cultures, certain older people are assigned elder status and their memories are accorded great respect.

Over the last few decades there has been the active promotion in some countries of reminiscence work—of old people sharing memories of life experiences in groups. This procedure contributes to the social health of a community in which older people are valued for their enduring memories of diverse life experiences, rather than being devalued because of a reducing ability to maintain recent memory abilities. An age-friendly society will affirm these abilities in older persons.

Key points

- As we get older, the most common change that we complain about is memory change.

- Knowledge about how memory changes as we get older is a lot more positive than in the past. Memory change with healthy ageing certainly doesn't interfere with everyday life in a dramatic way.

- Everyone is different, and the effect on memory of getting older is different for each person.

- Recent research describes the effect of getting older on attention processes, on the ability to get new information into storage, on the time that it takes to recall things, and on the 'tip of the tongue' experience.

- Recent research suggests that immediate memory and lifetime memory do not change as we get older

3

What else affects remembering? — health, attitude, lifestyle

In this section, we will use people's stories to illustrate the often complex interaction of physical and emotional factors that can affect memory abilities. Some of these are beyond our control: for example, a stroke can impact on our ability to remember, in an irreversible way. However, there are choices we can make, to do with health, lifestyle and emotional balance, that will help us get more out of our memory abilities.

How 'healthy' your memory is depends quite a bit on how healthy you are. Many people notice fluctuations in their ability to remember when they experience changes to their physical well-being—when they are hospitalised, after a general anaesthetic or during a severe cold.

We can find that our ability to remember is worse when we are experiencing emotional stresses; during menopause; during bereavement; or when we're leading a very active social life combined with heavy workload and complex relationships. Taking steps to deal with stress or excessive busyness can improve our remembering.

Our attitudes towards our memory are important. Negative expectations can become a self-fulfilling prophecy. If we think we have no control over our memory abilities, we may never take action.

The following four stories show how these kinds of things influence memory abilities. Each story is followed by an analysis and some suggestions for action so that we can get the best out of our brains!

·:◎:·· Story 1: Kathleen, 71

'My memory is letting me down—I'm starting to think I might have Alzheimer's Disease.'

I seem to be having memory lapses left, right and centre at the moment. I often wonder if I'll end up like Grandma Kemp. She didn't know who I was in the end.

My memory for things in my past seems to be OK, it's things that have happened more recently that I keep forgetting. I seem to be always losing things, and I keep forgetting the details of conversations. I'm sure that my daughter is concerned about me 'losing it'. Last week I forgot to take over the cake tin that she wanted to borrow, and the week before I had a complete blank when I tried to remember the name of her best friend's daughter.

This has been happening for at least six months; ever since my back flared up again really. The pain just won't go away. I suppose I should take my daughter's advice and get it checked again. I hate complaining to the doctor. There always seems to be something wrong with me of late. Of course, everything comes at once, doesn't it?—my arthritis has also been bad over the past few months.

I've been staying at home a lot more recently. It's more of an effort to get out now, with all the pain that I'm in. I'm much more comfortable at home in my comfy chair listening to the radio. I enjoy knitting and reading. Besides, it gets embarrassing when I keep forgetting. I work myself up so much about it—I just don't trust myself to remember any more. I can stay more relaxed if I avoid using my memory. I can still knit and cook. It's not as if I can't look after myself.

I did it again yesterday—I couldn't find my wallet anywhere. I went from room to room looking for it. I even checked to see whether I'd left it in the car. I worked myself up into a real panic—it had over $100 in it. I kept going over and over in my mind where I had used it last. I kept telling myself how stupid I am—and in the back of my mind, the fear of having Alzheimer's lingered on. Of course I found it this morning—guess where? In my handbag: the most logical place for it!

Kathleen's situation is an all-too-common one. There are many factors which add up and in particular combinations are influencing how her memory works for her:

Age

Kathleen is 71, and she describes some of the changes in remembering that many older people experience. The fact that Kathleen is having trouble getting new things into memory storage, and getting stored information—like names—out quickly, fits with the current research on memory and ageing. She also says that her memory for the past and for procedures like knitting and cooking is OK. This pattern of memory change fits well with what is known about age-related memory change.

Health (chronic pain)

Kathleen's difficulty with remembering may be exaggerated at the moment because of her health. She is in chronic pain, with arthritis and back trouble. When someone has constant pain, it often affects their ability to concentrate and pay attention. She may not, in fact, be 'forgetting' information—it may not be getting into her memory storage in the first place, because she has not paid adequate attention to it.

Attitudes (anxiety, negative expectation, poor self-confidence)

Kathleen has developed a **memory-anxiety spiral**. She is anxious about her memory abilities, so she notices every time she has a memory lapse. Each time she 'forgets' something, it gives her more support for her theory about losing her memory due to early Alzheimer's Disease, so—she gets more anxious; anxiety probably lowers her ability to concentrate and pay attention, so she seems to be getting more forgetful, and so more anxious.

Kathleen has developed **negative expectations** about her memory abilities. After some months of difficulty in remembering, she now does not expect to remember well, and calls herself put-down names like 'stupid'. She has little self-confidence when it comes to remembering, and subsequently little motivation to remember. She has started to avoid situations where she will have to use her memory abilities. She withdraws from social interactions, becomes more of a 'social recluse'. She now believes that her memory is poor. Sometimes, people's beliefs about themselves can become self-fulfilling prophecies.

' I believe therefore I am' : I think I will forget, so I do forget.

Researchers have shown that whether we assess ourselves as competent, or not, is one of the most important aspects of memory functioning in older adults. If you doubt your memory ability, you most likely tend to avoid situations where you will need to use your memory. You can then easily lose confidence and make your memory worse than it actually is. You don't lack ability—you lack self-confidence in using it!

If Kathleen continues to believe that she does not have a good memory, then she will feel her memory is worse than it actually is. It won't help her to 'catastrophise' and say things like 'I can't remember anything' or 'I'm stupid, I'm always forgetting things'.

Lifestyle (participation in 'thinking' activities)

Kathleen has altered her lifestyle over the past six months. While she is not interacting with different people in social living activities, she is not being challenged to think or reason about things. **Research has shown a strong association between good memory abilities and pursuit of a wide variety of activities that involve thinking and reasoning.** (However, this does not necessarily mean that good memory directly results from being active in social ways. It may be that the people whose memory functions well are also those who participate in many thinking activities.) Thinking may involve doing a crossword, listening to a complex discussion on radio, reading a book which challenges her beliefs—all on her own. Or she may find her thinking is better challenged by talking and even arguing with one or more people.

Participating in these kinds of activities could help her to feel more positive about herself and her capabilities. Feeling good about herself is definitely a good thing for memory function. When she values herself, she will achieve a personal affirmation of her ability.

Perhaps the best approach is to maintain a comfortable activity that stimulates the mind for her as an individual. There are many different ways to keep the mind active, not just the oft-cited things like crosswords, brain-teasers, learning a new language, chess and puzzles. Other ways to promote thinking include hobbies or jobs, reading, talking to people, meeting new people, going to the theatre, films, galleries, or on holidays, listening to music, fixing the car, gardening, learning new songs, new dance steps, writing stories, or teaching a grandchild old nursery rhymes—to name a few!

Kathleen would benefit from:

- knowing what are the expected memory changes with normal ageing;
- reassurance that in her case she does not have the type of memory difficulties that are suggestive of the early stages of Alzheimer's Disease (see Chapter 4);
- identifying some of the factors that she can control which may be exaggerating her memory problem at the moment;
- identifying and using appropriate pain management strategies, with particular attention to her back pain and arthritis;
- taking risks like returning to and maintaining her previous level of 'thinking' activities;
- finding new ways to engage in thinking.

Story 2: Andrew, 36

'I can't rely on my memory at the moment—it's all over the place.'

I used to have a fantastic memory. I certainly wouldn't describe it as fantastic these days. I just can't rely on it any more. I keep forgetting important details at work, and I'm afraid that other people will start to notice soon. The other day I ended up having two meetings scheduled at exactly the same time, because I had completely forgotten that I had agreed to one of them the week before. Not to mention the time a few weeks ago when my boss asked me to ring a client, and I only remembered that she had asked me to do so when she came in to check how the phone call had gone.

Work is dominating my life at the moment. I'm working six days a week, usually from 8 am to at least 7.30 pm each day. I often bring work home. I need to. How else will I prove to my boss that I should be the one who gets promoted to the new job coming up? Besides, we've had some major projects to get done before Christmas. My manager expects that we will stay back when we have deadlines for the big jobs. I can't be going home early when everyone else works late.

My girlfriend, Jane, is not happy with me. She's always complaining that I spend more time with my workmates than I do with her. There have been a few Christmas parties with our friends that I've had to pull out of at the last minute, because of work. I don't know what's going to happen with our relationship. All she does is complain. I think we've lost the spark. I just can't fit everything in to my life. I'm exhausted.

I used to be really fit. I was playing cricket every weekend this time last year. Of course, I've had to give that up this season. I couldn't make it to training two nights a week, and Saturday is one of the only days I get to see

Jane. It's annoying, because I know that when I'm fit, my energy levels are higher. If I could get some time to exercise, it would help me be less tired all the time.

So—I'm not fit, I'm skipping meals, and I would have to admit I've been hitting the grog more than usual of late. I have a few drinks when I'm entertaining clients at luncheons, and I usually have a few beers to unwind when I get home. Dinners these days are take-aways on the way home from work. I can't be bothered cooking when I get home so late. Jane keeps telling me I need to lose weight—and I know she is right.

Many people in Andrew's situation would begin to notice that their memory is not as reliable as it usually is. There are many aspects of Andrew's life that he can alter if he wants to get the most out of his memory.

Lifestyle (stress, workload, fatigue, relationship problems)

When Andrew says that his work is dominating his life, he could also say that it is dominating his memory. His heavy workload is leading to **stress** and **fatigue**. Memory lapses are often related to doing too much, especially doing too many things at once. Add exhaustion and stress to this, and you've got a pretty mean combination as far as memory goes! This combination would have a direct effect on his ability to concentrate and pay attention. Andrew has probably not 'forgotten' about his meeting and his phone call—he probably never got these bits of information into his memory filing cabinet in the first place, because he wasn't paying attention to them at the time.

Andrew is concerned about his relationship with Jane. This concern could also be reducing his ability to concentrate. The stress of relationship difficulties can often occupy our minds, and mean that it is difficult to take new information in.

Health (physical exercise, diet, alcohol)

The healthier you are, the better your memory will function. Andrew says that when he is physically fit, and participating in regular exercise, his energy level improves. If his energy level is higher, then he may be able to handle his workload and social commitments more easily. With less stress and fatigue, he should be able to concentrate and pay attention to things around him more easily. Of course this will have a positive effect on his memory.

At the moment, Andrew is not getting any regular **physical exercise**. He has given up sport because of work commitments. He also seems to have given up on the idea of healthy eating, which of course is critical to good health. His diet could certainly not be described as 'balanced'.

Andrew will need to watch his alcohol consumption. He says that he is having at least four alcoholic drinks a day at the moment. The current National Health and Medical Research Council (NHMRC) guidelines recommend that men have no more than four to six standard drinks a day, and women no more than two to four standard drinks a day. Any drink containing about 10 grams of alcohol—for example, one pot or middy (250–300 ml) of full-strength beer, one nip of spirits or one small glass of wine—is called a 'standard drink'. Andrew would not be thought of as a heavy drinker, but it could affect his health if he begins to drink in excess of these guidelines.

Our community is becoming increasingly aware of the effect of alcohol on health and on memory abilities. It is now a legal requirement in Australia for the labels of all alcoholic drinks to list the maximum number of standard glasses per bottle, which in turn indicates the approximate alcohol content of the drink. Heavy alcohol consumption is one of the most common causes of memory problems in middle-aged people, and excessive consumption may lead to memory problems in people of any age. If alcohol consumption regularly exceeds the NHMRC guidelines, it can cause real damage to the areas of the brain that are needed for memory functions. The direct effect of alcohol on the memory abilities of heavy drinkers may be compounded by nutritional deficiencies, psychiatric disorders, traumatic brain injury, vascular disease of the brain, cirrhosis of the liver, other diseases and other drug use.

Current research shows that if people who have been diagnosed as alcoholic cease drinking alcohol and maintain a balanced diet, their memory abilities may not have been permanently damaged. They usually first notice improvement to their level of attention or immediate memory ability. Slower improvement is seen in longer-term memory.

One drug that is sometimes thought to affect memory abilities is **marijuana**. The jury is still out on this question. Most research describes a transient effect on memory for 12-24 hours after use of marijuana. The research on more long-term effects on memory with chronic use of marijuana has shown no significant effects.

The effect of **combinations** of drugs—in particular, where drugs are used to alter mood is harder to assess, especially as variations in individual response may be even more marked than with single drugs. It is worth asking about the side effects of drugs, or the effects of drug combinations on memory abilities.

Attitudes (negative expectation and self-fulfilling prophecies)

Andrew appears to have given up on his memory. He says that it used to be 'fantastic', but now it is not, and so now he calls himself someone with an 'unreliable' memory. He is close to telling himself that it will always be so. If he expects to have memory lapses, then he might stop trying to remember, and so get into a self-perpetuating cycle.

Andrew would benefit from:

- realising that his memory ability is largely in his **control,** and that he can take action;
- not **labelling** himself as someone whose memory is permanently 'unreliable', but rather as someone whose memory is being affected by the situation he is currently in;
- using **memory strategies** as a back-up system, so that he believes that his memory will be reliable. If he doesn't already use a diary or electronic organiser, then he would be well advised to start doing so. Whenever he makes an appointment or is directed to do something, he could write it down in his diary.

He should also focus on

- **reducing his stress** at work, with good time management. If he can do this, his ability to concentrate and pay attention should improve, which could have a direct effect on his ability to remember. At work he will need to prioritise jobs, and work on one at a time. He will need to make a real effort to focus on the task at hand, not to let his mind wander on to other things, reduce any obvious distractions, and if he is interrupted while doing something, go back to it as soon as possible afterwards.

Finally, Andrew's goals should include

- **putting his health first,** rather than his work (but of course his work will benefit too)—improving his diet, limiting his alcohol intake, and making regular daily exercise for about 30 minutes part of his life; and

- taking steps to **discuss his relationship** concerns with Jane and work on the damaging conflicts that are emerging between them.

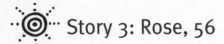 ## Story 3: Rose, 56

'Life is pretty lousy for me at the moment...my memory is hopeless!'

Life is pretty lousy for me at the moment. To top it all off, I had a really embarrassing phone call from the doctor's rooms this morning. I had forgotten my doctor's appointment at 9.30! I had really wanted to see him too, because I want to talk to him about the anti-depressants that he's put me on. I'm not sure if they are doing any good.

That's not the only thing I've forgotten. My memory is hopeless! Last week I forgot to pass on an important phone message to Jeff, my 23-year-old son, who is unemployed and living at home. It was about a possible job, and I just hope he hasn't missed out because of me.

I also forgot that Kim, my 26-year-old daughter, had changed my baby-sitting days this week. I usually look after her three-year-old daughter, and one-year-old son on Tuesdays, Wednesdays and Fridays. This week she arrived with them on Monday—I had completely forgotten that I had them for an extra day this week. Kim had a conference to attend.

My younger daughter, Fiona, moved out with her boyfriend about five months ago. I'm sure he's on drugs. I don't trust him. Of course, I can't say anything about it to her, but I worry. I hope she has enough sense not to try them. There's nothing that I can do about it really, but it worries me sick!

Life at home is fairly hectic these days. Bill, my husband, is at home during the day. He was made redundant from his work almost two years ago, and he just sits around and doesn't even work on the vegie garden any more. So I've got Bill and Jeff around the house all the time. Three days a week I've also got my grandchildren, Zoe and Nicholas, to look after.

I'm finding that I get tired very easily. I don't seem to have the energy that I used to have. I actually don't enjoy many of the things I used to enjoy either. I've lost interest in the garden. I look outside and see weeds every-where — but I don't seem to have the energy or desire to do anything about it. My day is taken up with chores for my family.

I don't sleep well. I keep getting these horrible hot flushes at night. I wake up soaked from perspiration. I suppose it's my menopause. I had my last period four years ago. I tried Hormone Replacement Therapy for a while, but I didn't like the idea of being dependent on a pill so I went off it. I often wonder if it's the menopause that is making my memory so hopeless.

Meanwhile, things with Bill are not fantastic. I get sick of having him around all the time, and having to do everything for him. I wish he would do more around the house. He has become very boring and we don't have fun together any more.

Rose thinks that her memory problem is part of menopause. While it is possible that menopause may be contributing to her difficulties, the main influence is probably her 'pretty lousy' situation at home. Most people would need enormous inner resources, a special strength of personality and much useful social support to avoid feeling depressed if they were living the life of this middle-aged woman. It is common for people to focus on a single medical problem as the cause of their memory difficulties, when in fact there are many other powerful factors which will remain in play unless they are identified.

Health (menopause, depression, medication side effects)

There is still little known about the effect that menopause has on memory although many women complain that their memory suffers.

Some women report that Hormone Replacement Therapy (HRT) improves their memory. Others are more specific—they say that HRT reduces insomnia (a common symptom of menopause) and therefore increases their ability to pay attention. Recent research into sleep deprivation reports it as having even more adverse effects on thinking abilities (and by implication, memory functioning) than an alcoholic hangover.[4] More work on the effects of changes in hormone levels on memory in post-menopausal women, and of long-term usage of HRT in older women, is much needed.

Rose describes some symptoms of depression, and is taking anti-depressants prescribed by her local doctor. People who have depression often remark that their memory is poor. Being depressed or preoccupied by stressful thoughts can certainly mean that it is difficult to concentrate and pay attention. This can, of course, affect the ability to get new information into memory storage. Rose appears to be very preoccupied with family issues, and her reduced energy and lack of enjoyment in things that she previously enjoyed suggest that she is depressed.

Depression is a condition that often requires medication to treat it. Many people notice that their memory improves with this treatment. However, others feel that anti-depressants have the reverse effect. Generally speaking, anti-depressant medications that have been developed over the past six years have fewer side effects, and less of an adverse effect on memory. It is always worth discussing with your doctor any side effects that you notice from any medication that you are taking. Everyone reacts differently to different medications, and alteration to memory abilities can occur as an unexpected side effect with some drugs.

Lifestyle (fatigue)

Rose sounds exhausted. She is not sleeping well, and her days are full of family commitments. She has demands from grandchildren, her own adult children and from her husband. Being so tired would not be helping her memory. The types of things that she is forgetting, and the fact that she is not able to concentrate and focus on information to be remembered, could easily be related to her fatigue. New information would often not get into her memory filing cabinet.

Attitudes (hopelessness)

Rose says '**My memory is hopeless**'. Every time she has a memory lapse, she uses this to strengthen her theory that her memory is hopeless. She blames the problem on menopause, and has given up on seeking ways to help her memory. With this attitude, her memory is not likely to get any better. She seems to think that she has no direct control over how well her memory can be made to work for her.

Rose would benefit from:

- acknowledging that there are some aspects of her life that she has the ability to control. If she works on these, she may find that her memory abilities improve.
- discussing her anti-depressant **medication** with her doctor, especially with regard to possible side effects on her memory;
- thinking about **other ways to manage her depression**;
- asking her daughter to organise alternative childcare arrangements for a while;
- discussing her **sleeping difficulty** with her doctor, and possibly getting a referral to a 'sleep specialist' who can outline different strategies that help to combat insomnia;

- allowing time each day to **do something for herself**;
- making time for 30 minutes of **moderate physical activity** a day;
- ensuring that she is eating a **well-balanced diet** which she enjoys!;
- using memory strategies as a 'back-up system' to get around her current difficulty with concentration and attention, to combat the feeling of 'hopelessness', and to show her that she can and already does remember many things;
- joining or even forming a women's self-help group to discuss management of mid-life changes—menopause, relationships, food and body pleasures!

Story 4: Richard, 67

'I thought his memory would get better after the stroke, but lately it has started to get worse.'

My husband, Richard, had a mild stroke about a year and a half ago. Ever since, he has had a slight problem with his memory. The specialists at the rehabilitation centre told us that this was due to the memory areas of the brain being affected in a mild way by his stroke.

He's OK when it comes to remembering things from the past. It's just remembering more recent things that he has trouble with. It has been a very subtle change, so that not many other people outside the family have noticed.

Over the last three months, I've noticed that the problem with his memory has gradually got worse. When I say this to him, he says 'It's from the stroke, and there's nothing I can do about it'. Unfortunately the stroke seems to have left him with that 'resigned to my fate' attitude. He is quite apathetic. The doctors told me that people's personalities can change in this way after a stroke.

We moved into a smaller unit about three months ago. Our house was getting to be too much for us to manage. The garden was large, and we just couldn't keep it to the standard we wanted. It was sad to leave the house that we had been in since we were married, but we just had to be practical.

Lately, I've noticed that Richard is asking me to repeat what I say to him quite often. I'm sure his hearing has got worse. When I think about it, it's usually things people tell him that he forgets. He also often asks me to tell him where things are around the unit. We've had to change where we keep most of our things, now that we're in a smaller place.

He had trouble with his throat—needing to clear it all the time and feeling an ache in his neck muscles, yet he didn't have a cold. A specialist thought his throat muscles were in strain and put him on Valium about six months ago, as a muscle relaxant. It seems to be helping with the muscular problem, but I wonder if it has any side effects on his memory? He seems to be less able to concentrate.

Sometimes I think I should get him to practise using his memory. Surely, if he has lots of practice at remembering, doing the same thing over and over again, it should make his memory get better.

I'll have to do something about this. The specialists told me he would get better with time, not worse.   Lilian

Richard's wife has reason to feel concerned. He does have real brain injury and a consequent memory problem due to the stroke, but the changes she has observed over the last three months are not likely to have the same cause. It looks as if other factors have come into play. Each person will have a quite individual style of response to a sudden trauma like a stroke, depending on their own personality and life experience. Even with brain damage in apparently the identical area, two people will not show the same personal approach to the experience.

These other factors can usually be addressed in some way, and a positive effect on remembering is often the result.

Health (brain injury, grief, fear, hearing impairment, side effects of medication)

Richard has been told that he sustained mild damage to the brain from his stroke, particularly in the areas that are needed for some aspects of memory function. The stroke has most likely caused limitations in his ability to get new information into storage, and to be able to recall it later.

There are many other causes of change to the memory areas of the brain, apart from strokes. For example, serious head injuries, certain forms of epilepsy and Parkinson's Disease are known to alter our ability to remember. Major operations can also sometimes have this effect. We will discuss the effect of Alzheimer's Disease in the following chapter. With any known brain condition, it is important to check continually for health, lifestyle and attitude factors that could be making the memory problem worse than it is.

It has also been mentioned that Richard's personality changed after the stroke. He became more apathetic. A lack of motivation, no matter what the cause, can affect remembering in a negative way. If you are not motivated to remember something, then you are less likely to get it into your memory filing cabinet.

Richard may have some grief issues, which are not obvious to his wife. He has suffered some real losses due to his stroke, and has also recently moved from the house he lived in since he was married, which for some people can be a major loss. Grief and adjustment to loss can affect people's ability to concentrate and pay attention. New information may not get into memory storage, because attention was not paid to it.

People who have a stroke—particularly if they have seen it happen to someone else—are likely to experience fear. This fear can have a psychologically quite paralysing effect on some, such that there is a withdrawal from social interaction, depression and apparent apathy. Lilian may need some guidance in how to talk about it with Richard.

Richard's hearing may be another factor that is affecting his ability to get new information into storage. If you don't hear something, then it will not go into your immediate memory storage for processing. This means that the information will not get into your more enduring storage files. It is important to be aware of the effect of sensory loss on memory. Our senses of hearing, vision, smell, touch and taste are important to the processes of remembering.

It is worth checking any medications for their possible side effects on memory abilities. Valium (Diazepam) is a commonly used drug and is known to have a negative effect on remembering. As is the case with Rose, recognition of side effects of a drug can influence how long it needs to be taken and even the dosage.

Lifestyle (unfamiliar environment)

Richard's memory started to get worse at about the same time as he and his wife moved into their new unit. Being in a new or unfamiliar environment can make remembering more difficult, especially for people with any damage to the brain. When you move house, there is so much that is new to you. Learning where everything is kept can be a major undertaking, particularly when you have lived in your previous house for a very long time.

Attitude

Richard's wife wonders whether she can help him to improve his memory by getting him to use it over and over again, and practise often, but Richard does not seem open to self-help suggestions. He says 'It's from the stroke, and there's nothing I can do about it'. While he holds a non-motivated attitude he will probably not actively seek out any advice or benefit from any suggested tasks. Moreover, given the period of time since Richard's stroke, it's unlikely that he would be able to restore lost memory abilities with repetitive practice. Thinking of specific strategies for everyday situations that he will come across is likely to be more effective (see Chapter 5).

Lilian will benefit from discussing her feelings and attitudes towards Richard with an experienced counsellor.

Richard would benefit from:

- **being reviewed by his doctor** to check if any medical complications are causing his memory to get worse;
- knowing that there are some factors that are **under his control** that could be adding to his memory problem at the moment;
- asking his doctor about **possible side effects of Valium** (Diazepam), and any possible alternative treatment for his throat muscle spasm;
- asking his doctor to **check his hearing**, and finding out if he would benefit from a hearing aid;
- joining a group, or having responsibility for tasks or decisions about the house—these may act as motivators;
- having Lilian or friends face him when they are telling him something they want him to hear (and remember).

Key points

- Our ability to remember can fluctuate from time to time.

- Our memory abilities are influenced by various factors, some of which are under our own control.

- These factors include our health, our lifestyle and, importantly, our attitudes and beliefs in our own skills.

- To get the most out of our memories, it is important to be aware of these factors, and if necessary to actively do something about them.

4

Could it be
Alzheimer's ...?

Alzheimer's Disease has received a great deal of media attention over recent years. It is often the first explanation that occurs to people who notice some type of memory loss in themselves or someone they know. Because more people than ever before are living to 80- or 90-something, younger people are now more likely to have first-hand experience of someone with Alzheimer's Disease. This, in combination with the idea that Alzheimer's Disease could be inherited, has caused widespread anxiety as a condition of ageing.

'I'm 76 now and I've noticed that my memory is not as reliable as it used to be, I often wonder if I'm developing dementia.'

'I've just turned 50 and I keep forgetting where I've put things—could it be the beginnings of Alzheimer's Disease?'

If we forget something when we are younger we might call ourselves 'scatterbrained', but if we forget something when we are older, we start to call ourselves 'senile' and other quite unpleasant names!

For many of us, the possibility of developing dementia is one of the greatest fears of growing old. After all, memory is self. Fortunately, dementia is not a part of normal ageing: only 4 in 10 000 (0.04%) people under 65 have Alzheimer's Disease,[5] and in the 65-75 age range the figure is still less than 6 per cent. However, the percentage does rise with increasing age—to something like 16 per cent for those aged 80-84.[6]

When younger people are concerned about their memory it usually turns out to be something apart from dementia that is the cause of the problem—most commonly depression, anxiety, or a heavy workload.

My father is 54 years old, and is one of the most fit and healthy people I know. He migrated to Australia some 30 years ago, with no knowledge of the English language and maybe fourth-grade education. Now he works for one of the largest retail organisations in Australia, travelling around the state, training others in his area of expertise. He is very easy-going and very social, but there is one thing that seems to worry him at times: his memory. He worries about it because his mother had Alzheimer's Disease before she died five or six years ago.

The things he says he forgets are names, phone numbers, dates and sometimes things that family members have told him in passing. I'm 25 years old and have the same forgetfulness—if I don't write things down, I might as well have never been told. My father is also partially deaf in one ear, so chances are he may not have even heard something that he thinks he has forgotten. And, while his grasp of the English language is very good, he sometimes misses things if a person speaks too quickly, or uses uncommon words or has a thick or unusual accent. He leads a full and busy life and has many things on his mind at any time—one would expect to forget the things he forgets!

But when I tell him this it serves only to ease his mind until the next time he can't remember something that I told him. And then what overpowers him is that his mother died of Alzheimer's Disease, and that he can't remember something. **Ellen**

 ## What is dementia?

We hear many words used to describe the existence of progressive decline in mental abilities, and this can be confusing. One of the most common terms is 'senility', which is usually directly associated with old age ('He's going senile'). Other terms that you might have heard are 'dementia', 'senile dementia', 'Alzheimer's Disease', 'multi-infarct dementia', and 'vascular dementia'. 'Dementia' is a better term than 'senility', since it can encompass the small number of people who develop progressive memory loss in their earlier years.

One way to think about dementia is to see it as evidence of a change of brain functioning. It can have many different causes, just as a high temperature is a sign of body change that could stem from a variety of illnesses.

The most common sign of dementia is progressive memory loss. It is accompanied by decline in other areas of mental ability, which adversely affects a person's ability to function in everyday life.

My wife has just been diagnosed with Alzheimer's Disease. Over the past three years her memory has gradually gone from bad to worse. She always had a good memory, but now things just don't sink in—I answer her questions and she asks me the same thing again straight away. She forgets where things are kept around the house and keeps putting them in new locations, and of course can't find them later. She has been lost on several occasions in shopping centres. Now her memory for the past is slipping too. The other day someone asked her what her job was when she was younger, and she couldn't tell them. She also forgets the names of plants that she used to know so well. When she can't think of a word she says 'thingamy', and sometimes its hard to know what she is talking about. I've also noticed that she puts on the same clothes day after day. She used to be so meticulous about her appearance. Thank goodness she can still play solo and do crosswords. It's nice to see her enjoying herself.   Jack

There are other causes of dementia, but 'Alzheimer's Disease' is the most common. About 70 per cent of all cases of dementia are related to Alzheimer's Disease.[7] So, in fact, when we say the words 'Alzheimer's Disease' and 'dementia', we are usually meaning the same thing.

What causes dementia apart from Alzheimer's Disease?

The next most common cause is damage from extensive small strokes (sometimes called 'multi-infarct dementia' or 'vascular dementia'), arising from problems with the blood supply to the brain. People often don't notice when they have them, but a succession of minor strokes can affect memory and other thinking abilities. In a much smaller number of cases, dementia may be related to other conditions, such as Parkinson's Disease, Huntington's Disease, long-term alcoholism, AIDS and rare degenerative diseases of the brain.

We will therefore concentrate on Alzheimer's Disease, as this is the most common cause of dementia, and is the focus of a lot of anxiety in people concerned about memory losses.

 ## What causes Alzheimer's Disease?

We know that Alzheimer's Disease is a result of brain-cell malformations and chemical changes in the brain, but we still don't know what actually causes these processes to happen in people's brains.

Many potential causes are being explored. A great deal of research has been conducted on genetics and Alzheimer's Disease. There is still no clear answer about the inheritability of the disease. If one or more of your relatives have had Alzheimer's Disease, it is not possible to predict the likelihood of your developing the disease, and your chances are not necessarily increased because you have had the disease in your family.

Environmental risk factors have also been explored in detail. Current research indicates that you don't need to throw out all your aluminium saucepans. Results of studies investigating the role of excess aluminium remain inconclusive.

 ## At what age are you most likely to develop Alzheimer's Disease?

The proportion of people developing Alzheimer's Disease increases with age, but the vast majority of older people do not develop the disease. A higher proportion of people in their eighties develop

Alzheimer's Disease, but even in this age group, approximately eight out of every ten people, or the vast majority, have no signs of the illness. Men and woman develop Alzheimer's Disease in equal proportions—although it seems that women have it more, this is because more women than men live to an advanced age at present.

Is there a cure for Alzheimer's Disease?

A great deal of the current research into Alzheimer's Disease is focusing on potential treatments, but so far no medical cure has been discovered.

Stop-press announcements about possible new treatments for Alzheimer's Disease hit the headlines from time to time. Most new discoveries require much investigation over many years before they can be transformed into procedures, drugs or preventative behaviours. The drugs that are currently available are designed to slow down the progression of memory loss (see below), but they do not stop it.

With no cure available for Alzheimer's Disease at present, management involves ensuring maximum quality of life for the person with dementia, and the provision of considerable support for carers. There is no doubt that other factors (see Chapter 3) can exacerbate the symptoms of dementia, so good health remains a priority.

Can drugs improve memory?

People with and without dementia often ask about the use of drugs to enhance memory abilities. Some people use old remedies such as Gingko Biloba and other herbal or homeopathic treatments, or even fish oil. Research on these treatments has not been widely reported in the scientific literature. The use of Vitamin E to slow the progression of memory loss in those with Alzheimer's Disease is currently being investigated, with reports of early success. We will hear a lot more about this in the near future.

We are beginning to hear more and more about the so-called 'smart drugs'—drugs that are specifically promoted as enhancing memory functions. Some are currently available, but most remain at the preliminary research stage. These drugs work on chemicals in the brain that are used in the memory processes.

Tacrine (or Cognex) and Donepezil (or Aricept) are two drugs that appear to slow the progression of memory loss in the early stages of Alzheimer's Disease. Donepezil is reported to have less harmful side effects: it causes mild and transient side effects, including nausea, diarrhoea and vomiting in a small number of people, whereas Tacrine has been noted to cause liver damage in some people. Donepezil is now recommended for people in the early stages of Alzheimer's Disease who are otherwise physically healthy and have a carer to supervise the administration of the tablets.

Research has focused on the effect of these drugs on rats and on people who have Alzheimer's Disease. At this stage little or no research has been done with people who do not have Alzheimer's Disease. Doctors are unlikely to recommend drugs for the wider population who do not show signs of Alzheimer's Disease and may wish to use them for memory enhancement. We simply don't know enough about them yet. But we will hear a lot more about the development of 'smart drugs' in the near future.

*The primary scientific literature does not justify the claim that smart drugs can be of any therapeutic or memory-boosting value to **healthy humans**.
(emphasis added)* Steven Rose[8]

How is Alzheimer's Disease diagnosed?

There are many different pathways towards an assessment for possible dementia. The most usual procedure (it will vary from state to state, country to country) involves investigation by a local doctor, who may refer the client to a specialist in the diagnosis and management of memory problems. Such specialists may be members of teams in memory clinics.

When someone is diagnosed as having Alzheimer's Disease, it is said to be a 'diagnosis of exclusion'—that is, all other conditions that could be causing the person's memory problems have been ruled out or excluded. If no other reason for the memory problem can be found, then it is diagnosed as Alzheimer's Disease.

Recent press reports have pointed towards new discoveries that may soon make it possible to say who is going to develop Alzheimer's Disease. However, with no present cure for the disease, many people would ask 'Would I want to know?' and 'Would it enhance my life?'.

Other conditions which can cause short- and long-term changes in memory functioning include vitamin deficiencies, stroke, tumour, infections and many other illnesses. Investigations performed to check for these include a physical examination, blood tests, and brain scans such as CT (Computerised Tomography) or MRI (Magnetic Resonance Imaging) scans. These can be organised by a local doctor or specialist, to be done at a hospital or special pathology centre.

What is involved in memory assessment or testing?

A typical memory clinic in Australia is based in a metropolitan hospital and has a team which may include geriatricians, psychiatrists, social workers, occupational therapists, speech pathologists, nurses and neuropsychologists. People are usually referred to the clinic by their local doctor. The person who is reported to have the memory disorder is seen by one of the doctors, and the person's family is interviewed by a team member to gather information about how and when the memory problem developed. This is important because those with the memory difficulties are often not able to give exact details concerning the nature and extent of their own problem. More detailed assessment of the person is often carried out, typically followed by feedback for the person and the family. The person is usually seen at the clinic again in about a year's time. This follow-up allows the medical team to check the diagnosis and to discuss ongoing management.

This type of memory clinic does not charge fees, because it is part of a public health service. If a private practitioner service is chosen, the fees are set by that clinician's professional body.

As well as tests of physical status, an assessment of memory and other mental abilities is also performed. This can vary from simple tests to more detailed neuropsychological assessment. A doctor will often use brief tests of memory, which are useful because they are quick and easy to use, and interpreting them does not require extensive training. However, they do not always pick up mild or subtle memory impairment; and if they do, they may not yield enough information for the tester to discover the cause of the memory problem. Nor do they examine a person's memory in enough detail to be helpful with planning for future care. Sometimes a doctor will refer on for more comprehensive assessment of memory—by a neuro-psychologist, for instance .

How is Alzheimer's Disease different from normal memory loss?

Delys' case will help to answer this question. Prior to her retirement (at the age of 65), Delys was concerned at how her memory abilities had seemed to deteriorate, and she was anxious about her future as an old woman. She consulted a neuropsychologist (Anne), who carried out memory testing to use as a reference point for her memory in later years. The assessment did not reveal any signs of Alzheimer's Disease. There were four main reasons for this conclusion.

First of all, there was Delys' awareness of and focus on these changes. A few of the people who go on to develop Alzheimer's Disease are aware of the changes in their memory in the early stages, but most of them are not, whereas people with everyday memory complaints are often very conscious of them. For example, they complain of difficulty remembering people's names, trouble thinking of specific words and not being able to find things. They can relate in great detail all the things that they have forgotten recently, and they tend to remember every instance accurately!

Second, Delys' memory abilities tended to fluctuate, whereas in Alzheimer's Disease, the problems in remembering are usually there all the time. She was generally able to remember things if she concentrated hard on doing so. Someone with Alzheimer's Disease would find this more difficult.

Third, the tests showed that she was not experiencing any problems with other areas of intellect and language abilities. Even in early

Alzheimer's Disease, most people show problems with some aspects of language or intellectual processing.

Lastly, there were other factors in Delys' lifestyle that could explain the changes that she was noticing in her memory—the dramatic alteration in her routine, and her heavy workload.

Everyday memory problems can be frustrating, but they don't pose a threat to your ability to function independently. People with Alzheimer's Disease often require assistance with everyday activities that they used to do by themselves. They might forget how to do things that they have always been very good at (for example, where to post a letter, how to knit, or how to write a cheque). They sometimes cannot remember the names of close relatives, or they may get lost while driving on a familiar route.

Fluctuations in day-to-day remembering are often the result of not paying close attention. People often notice that they can still learn something new if they are interested enough, and make an effort. Many people find that their memory plays more tricks on them when they are in a new setting, or when they are under pressure for health or lifestyle reasons, as described in Chapter 3.

Does an 'all clear' now mean I won't get Alzheimer's Disease in the future?

An assessment like Delys' doesn't predict the future; it simply shows that the changes in memory abilities are not typical of Alzheimer's Disease and points to the most likely causes of the memory problem at the time. Repeating the assessment after one or two years to monitor any change would be useful. The memory loss in Alzheimer's typically gets worse with time.

Can I tell if someone else has Alzheimer's Disease?

We have outlined some areas where the memory change of those with Alzheimer's Disease is different to the problems of everyday memory functioning; but it isn't a clear boundary. In fact, knowing whether memory change is part of normal ageing or a sign of oncoming dementia is one of the more difficult diagnostic challenges for memory specialists.

This book will certainly not provide enough information to allow people to work out whether they have Alzheimer's Disease or not. Nor can a memory specialist make conclusions from single instances of memory loss. If someone says, 'My father repeats himself in the same conversation—do you think he has dementia?', it would not be possible to answer him with certainty. People with and without dementia repeat themselves in conversation. One would need to know more about how often it happens, under what circumstances, how long it has been happening for. A comprehensive physical and memory assessment might be the best course if it were a real concern for the person.

When to seek help and where

If you have considered other influences on memory abilities and you remain concerned, then it is best to seek further advice. See 'What to read and where to go', p. 127.

The best first step would be your local doctor. Your doctor can refer you to the appropriate specialists if necessary.

Key points

• For many of us, the possibility of developing dementia is one of the greatest fears of getting old. Younger people sometimes have similar concerns.

• The proportion of people who develop Alzheimer's Disease increases with age, but the vast majority of people *do not* develop the disease.

• When we say the words 'Alzheimer's Disease' and 'dementia', we mean essentially the same thing. Alzheimer's Disease is by far the most common, but not the only, cause of dementia.

• Current research into Alzheimer's Disease is focusing on potential treatments for the disease, but so far *no medical cure* has been discovered.

• If you or someone that you know has been having memory problems lately—first consider the variety of adverse influences on memory function that we discussed in Chapter 3, before you jump to the conclusion that the problem is Alzheimer's Disease.

• If you remain concerned, then it may be best to seek further advice. The best first step would be to consult your family doctor.

5

Some useful memory strategies

People use their memory for many different things. Some use it at work, some are actively learning something new, and others place little demand on their brains to learn any new things at all. Attitudes also vary. Some people think that their memory is OK, but would like to find some new ways to get the most out of it. Others may think that their memory is not working as well as it should be, and would like to know why, and what they can do.

Possible reasons for memory change

In Chapter 3 we ran through some factors that can lead to memory function not being at its best. It may be useful to consider how these factors could apply to you. Run through this checklist now, and mentally note any on the list that you think might be having an adverse effect on your memory ability at the moment.

- Do you have low expectations about how your memory will work for you?
- Are you taking any medication, and if so, do you know if it can affect your memory?
- Is your vision impaired in any way?
- Is your hearing impaired in any way?
- Do you have any chronic pain?
- Could your hormone levels be altered at the moment?
- Do you think you might be depressed or often 'down in the dumps'?
- Are you experiencing a high level of anxiety, fear or distress?
- Is your workload too heavy?
- Do you drink much alcohol, or use other drugs to excess?
- Is the level of your mental stimulation adequate for you?
- Are you eating, exercising and sleeping well?

To get the most out of your memory you may need to take action. You may need to change your thoughts about yourself and your memory. Having realistic rather than negative expectations about memory functioning can help you to be more relaxed about it. A change in what you think and what you say to yourself can actually enhance your memory abilities.

Many factors can reduce your capacity to attend to what is going on around you. It may be this **reduction in attention** that is having an effect on your memory abilities at the moment. You may need to find ways to increase your attention to what you want to get into your memory storage.

If you think that your **workload** could explain why your memory is not at its best, then consider ways to reduce it. Think about time management, pace yourself, and include brief times to properly relax, at your desk, in the car park, at the bus stop. Being relaxed has a positive effect on your attention level. You might like to investigate some specific relaxation techniques from the wide literature on stress management, such as deep-muscle relaxation, meditation, breathing and yoga.

Your **health** can affect your ability to pay attention. Do you need to have your vision or hearing checked? Do you have pain that needs to be investigated?

At a time when there was much going on in my life, new course [of study], new relationship, new part-time work, I was asked by my brother to deliver an item the following day. I completely forgot, I did not even have an inkling of remembering what he requested. Combining this incident with another soon after, where I totally forgot to meet up with a friend, I fell into a tailspin. I thought 'I'm losing my mind', 'What's wrong with me?' I was just 26 at the time.   Peter

Dealing with memory change

We have discussed the current opinions about the effect of increasing age on different types of memory in Chapter 2. We know that for many older people the main area of difficulty is in getting new information into storage and then getting it out quickly and completely when it is wanted. These changes can be very frustrating, but we can learn to accommodate them in the same way as we would safeguard our bodies if skiing, sailing or playing squash as older persons. We can do this by allowing more time for mental processing: time for paying attention, for testing out the best new strategies to assist us and time for practising recall of new information.

Acknowledging and adapting to memory change in this way is an important and healthy adaptation to increasing age, but we can do more; we can also learn to make use of memory aids or strategies to lessen the impact on our lives and thus feel more in control. Most of us use them without realising it, for getting new information into the files, and also for getting old information out from that often over-flowing mental filing cabinet containing files for memories about children, spouse, parents, home, study and numerous others. Some are simple, some quite involved.

Memory aids or strategies can be divided into two types. **Internal memory strategies** are the ones that come from within us and involve some sort of thinking: some mental manipulation. For example, to remember where you left your wallet, you might mentally retrace your steps since you last used it. **External memory strategies** involve using some sort of external aid to help memory, for example, a note pad for writing a shopping list on, or a diary. They can also involve making changes to your external surroundings: for instance, you might put an item near the front door so that you remember to take it with you when you leave.

We will now run through some examples of both external and internal strategies. When we drew up this list, we found that one thing often led to another. We talked to people about what strategies they use, and discovered some creative and ingenious ideas. When you read through our suggestions, they may prompt you to add your own. You might remember strategies that you haven't used for a while, or come up with variations on the ones that we have included. Our list is by no means exhaustive—think of it as a starting point.

 ## Internal memory strategies

The most common internal memory strategies involve three main features:

- **focusing attention**
- **adding meaning** to the information that you want to remember
- **reducing the amount of information** to be remembered

These strategies are especially useful for older people since paying attention to many aspects of the information to be remembered is what many people have difficulty with as they get older.

Some experts favour more elaborate techniques, such as mnemonics, so we will also run through examples of these and discuss their usefulness.

Focusing attention

We often say that we have 'forgotten' something when what we really mean is that we didn't get it into the 'filing cabinet' in the first place, because we didn't attend to it. **Fluctuating attention is one of the most common explanations for fluctuating memory abilities**.

For instance, you might not remember what your friend was wearing at dinner the night before, because you were paying attention to the interesting dinner guest sitting next to you, rather than to your friend's outfit; or you might not remember the name of the person you are introduced to before you make a speech, because you did not pay attention to it—you were too anxious about the speech.

Of course, we can't expect to pay attention to **everything** in our environment. We all have a mental 'rubbish bin' where information that we don't need or want to know about gets dumped. We remember things that are important to us much better than things which we consider unimportant. For instance, some of us enjoy learning how to fix our own car, while others are happy for someone else to remember how to fix it!

When there is something important to remember and we want to focus our attention on it, it helps to **reduce any distractions**. Turn the radio down, ask the kids to be quiet or turn the television off. Focus on one thing at a time wherever possible.

I work in sales and marketing—so I've trained myself to learn people's names. I'm better doing this at work than socially. I focus and make a real effort to put it in, and rid myself of distractions. Socially, I don't make the effort, I let myself be distracted.   Ron

How often do you meet someone for the first time, and not actually hear them say their name? Maybe you are nervous, or distracted by other thoughts, or things around you. You might be so focused on whether your gear is too way out for this occasion that you totally miss their name. The problem here is not one of forgetting, it is in 'getting the information in'. If you listen carefully to the person's name when you first meet them, you will have a better chance of remembering it later. If you don't hear the name, don't be afraid to say 'I didn't hear your name clearly...'.

In general it is helpful to make a **conscious effort** to attend to the key aspects of the new information you want to get into your memory files, such as the name of a person that you are being introduced to.

The best way for me to remember where my car is located in a large car park, is to concentrate on landmarks close to my car, like the floor number, or the colour of a nearby feature. I also look behind me as I am walking away from my car, and concentrate on how my car, and the landmarks around it, will look when I come back to it.   **Mary**

One of my friends shared her confusion at carefully remembering the '8' sign beside her car, and on return to the '8' sign realised they were speed signs which were everywhere ... and on every floor!   **Delys**

Rehearsal and repetition   Rehearsal and repetition are common strategies which help us to focus attention. Repetition involves repeating information out loud, whereas rehearsal is done in our heads.

For many of us, rehearsal and repetition are good strategies for remembering names. It can help even more if we stage the timing of our mental rehearsals. To do this, you gradually increase the amount of time between rehearsals. You might even rehearse the information again the next day. And remember to give yourself a bonus for being such a skilled rememberer! (Even telling someone, with pride, that you are a good rememberer can assist you continuing to be so in the future.)

I find that the best way for me to remember someone's name is to repeat it to myself three times after I have heard it.   **Angela**

Reinforcing rehearsal with repetition is useful. You can ask someone to repeat their name by saying, for example, 'Would you mind telling me your name again, I would like to get it right', 'Could you spell your name?', or 'How do you pronounce your name correctly?'. People are often pleased that you are making an effort to learn their name.

Using the name in the ensuing conversation often makes it easier to remember later on.

The only way that I can remember a name is if I keep saying it during conversation! I might say 'I'm glad to meet you, Jonathon', and later I usually use the name when I say goodbye.   **Tony**

Remember learning poems at school? We did this by repeating them over and over again until they were memorised. Some say this is a great way to remember jokes. Tell the joke to someone else straight away—tell it on as many different occasions as possible.

Do you ever wonder whether you have turned the iron or the oven off, or shut a window? Maybe you wonder if you locked a door when you left the house. Some people suggest that it helps to say out loud what you are doing at the time, so you might say 'I've turned the iron off', to yourself or to someone else. Sometimes the simple act of talking can increase your attention enough to make you remember what you have done or not done.

Adding meaning

As we discussed in Chapter 1, scientists think that how well we remember something depends on how deeply we process the information. If we attend to as many aspects as possible of the information to be remembered, then this 'deep' processing should help us to remember it later.

Deliberately being alert to and using the senses can help: for example, to remember a particular rose, focus on feeling its thorns, seeing its colour and shape, smelling its fragrance, while saying its name. Some say that it also helps to **make a judgement** about what we are wanting to remember. Do you like it or not? How does it make you feel? Or you can make a conscious link with a piece of information already stored. You might want to think to yourself how unusual a person's name is, or how the name reminds you of someone you knew when you were at school. You could also see what it looks like when it is written down. Can you get a special meaning from the name? For instance, if you can remember that your friend's children both have names that start with L, you might find it easier to recall that the names are Luke and Louise. (Of course there will be those who will tell you of their embarrassment at remembering the judgement or the comparison, but not the name itself!)

Common techniques that add meaning to the information to be remembered are associating and visualising. Some people use rhymes or acrostics to add meaning in a particular way. We will now outline these techniques.

Making associations Associating new information with something that we already know well is one way to add meaning to what we want to remember. You will probably find that if you connect or associate a name you have just heard with someone who has the same name and whom you know well, then the name is easier to remember. You might sometimes associate the new name with a famous personality too. Who you were with, where you were standing and the time of the day when you were told the name of a particular rose may help you to recall it when someone admires it in your garden next spring!

I have had people tell me that they remembered my unusual name by connecting it with 'delicious', and another, with 'Dallas', Texas, and another with 'delays'!   **Delys**

Another way to associate information is to connect something you want to remember to do with something that happens regularly around the same time. For example, you might associate taking your medication with mealtimes, or with cleaning your teeth at night. Thus something that you already do on a regular basis will trigger your memory for something else that you have to do.

Association is also useful to increase our knowledge in a certain area. The more that you know about a particular thing or issue, the easier it is to learn more about it. This is because you have more memory files on which that knowledge is based and thus it is easier to make new associations.

I'm very good at remembering the names of trees since I've got a background in forestry—but things that don't interest me, like fish for example, I simply don't recall.   **Toby**

In this way, getting new information into our files can be easier because we have a good range of knowledge stored in the past to link new ideas to. Filing is easier. We don't have to create a new folder each time, because we can put new files into already well-established folders.

The more I learn about plant names, the easier it is for me to remember new ones. The other day I saw a plant that I wanted to buy, so I looked up its botanical name. It was a Wattle, and I already knew that 'acacia' was the term for Wattle. It had purple growth tips, and I knew the word for that is 'purpurea'. The only new part that I had to remember was 'Baileyana'. This was easy, because I have a friend named 'Anna Bailey'.

If I hadn't known the terms for 'wattle' and 'purple', then I would have needed to remember three words, instead of just one!   **Anne**

As mentioned in Chapter 2, older people can draw on their life skills and developed wisdom to ensure effective learning. Experts in particular fields can use association to their advantage so that they can perform as well as, if not better than, younger novices who may be motivated and able to think fast.

Using associations can also be useful to help us get information out of our storage files; we can use them as cues. One type of cueing strategy that we often use is called a 'logical search'. This can be useful for those frustrating 'tip of the tongue' experiences, when we know that we have a word or name somewhere in our storage files, but cannot get it out when we want it! Especially difficult are proper names—like names of authors, actors or hotels that you have visited. In this situation a logical search would involve running through the letters of the alphabet, and thinking of possible names or words that begin with each letter.

People may also use sounds or smells to cue for information from a storage file. As outlined in Chapter 1, the use of 'filing tabs' in our memory filing cabinet can assist us in locating a particular file when we want it.

Contextual cues are also useful for 'tip of the tongue' experiences. Many people find that it helps to think of the situation where they first remembered the name or word. For remembering a name, you could think about where you last saw the person and any details about your conversation. Some say it is also helpful to think about the mood you were in. Recreating the context in your mind can make it easier to re-establish some connections, and get the word or name out of your storage files.

I had been trying for a long time to remember the family name of a girl that I went to school with, over 50 years ago. Usually I take great pride in my ability to remember names, but this one was getting to me. It was funny how I did eventually come to remember the name. I visualised the area where I grew up, and where my school was. All of a sudden it came to me, the name that I had been searching for, jumped back into my mind all of its own.   **Clive**

The use of action or location cues has also been suggested to help remember the location of something that is lost (e.g. your wallet). You can mentally retrace your steps—go through step by step what you did, where you were after that and where you last saw the thing. For instance, 'Where did I put the mail?—I collected it from the letter box, I came inside, I put my keys on the sideboard, I went into the kitchen to put the milk in the fridge...Aaaah! I left the mail on top of the fridge.' It can also help to actually return to the last place that you were in.

Sometimes I walk into a room and forget what I was going to say. If I go back to where I came from—voila!—the words that I was going to say miraculously appear.   **Graham**

If you can't remember where you have put something, you could pretend that you are putting the thing away for the first time and think of the likely places you would put it. How many of us go into a room to get something and forget what we've gone in to get! If you find yourself in this situation, you could think back, or actually go back, to the place where you first decided to do the thing.

Visualising   Another way to process information at a 'deeper' level and add meaning to it is to visualise it—to picture something in your mind, or create an image of the thing to be remembered. The power of visualisation is reflected in the old Chinese proverb, 'One seeing is worth ten thousand tellings'—or the modern saying, 'A picture is worth a thousand words'.

I have one memory trick that I was taught in primary school, yet whenever I tell anyone they look at me as if I'm crazy. I was told that an easy way to remember how to spell accommodation was to imagine booking two double rooms—hence the double 'c' and the double 'm'. Silly? It works for me!
Marion

Some people say that the more unusual or funny the image, the more they will remember it. Visualisation is a strong tool to use for some people, and can provide a very quick way of remembering. As with all powerful tools, it needs to be handled with great care or it can have somewhat explosive results...as Ethel recounts below.

A group of Senior Citizens took off on a mystery bus trip. We headed up towards the NSW border passing through one of the small towns around Echuca. Somewhere we stopped for morning tea and a walk to stretch our legs. We wandered into an opportunity shop, about fifteen of us.

As soon as I walked through the door the lady behind the counter beamed at me. I gave her a faint smile. We wandered about the shop and each time I looked across at the counter she beamed at me. Finally I said to my friend, 'Is there something funny about me?' She replied, 'No, don't worry about it'.

We then went to the counter to pay for our goods. The lady behind the counter said, 'Hello, Ethel—I haven't seen you in years.' I was stunned at the use of my name. I could not place this pleasant woman. She said to me, 'Think back to...' and she mentioned the local suburb where I had lived in the 1950s. The 'green light' went on, but I still could not remember her name. I had a mental picture—putting my hands some distance in front of my breasts, I said in a very loud voice, 'Oh, you're the lady with the enormous boobs!' The whole shop was silent for two seconds—then everyone, including the lady concerned, burst out laughing. We had a good chat about the old days. I don't think I'll ever forget her name again! And I know what you mean, Anne, about the power of visualisation being a strong cue to remembering.   **Ethel**

Rhymes   Many of us can remember nursery rhymes from our child-hood days. Making a rhyme about information to be remembered is another internal strategy which involves adding meaning to the information to be remembered. When we asked groups of people to recall early learnt rhymes, the most frequently remembered were: 'Thirty days hath September, April, June, and November, all the rest have 31, except February alone which has 28 days clear and 29 in each leap year'—and the not-so-well-known version—'Thirty days hath September, all the rest I don't remember'!

Some used yet another version of this. If you say the months of the year, with the aid of your trusty knuckle bones, you will always know how many days each month has. Put your closed fists together, to make a row of knuckles. Start with January, by touching the knuckle furthest to the left. February is the space between the knuckles. March is the next knuckle, and so on. July and August both fall on knuckles—there is no space between them. All the months which fall on a knuckle have 31 days!

'I before e except after c' is another rhyme in common use by English speakers, although this one is not 100 per cent reliable!

Acrostics   Acrostics are sometimes used to add meaning to information that we want to remember. To do this the first letter of each word on a list is used to make up a sentence.

Anyone who has learnt music is probably familiar with the following acrostics: 'Every Good Boy Deserves Fruit'—the lines of the treble staff, E, G, B, D, F; and 'All Cows Eat Grass'—the notes on the spaces of the bass staff, A, C, E, G.

Do you know what this acrostic is used to remember?

'Richard Of York Gains Battles In Vain'*

People are able to be creative with acrostics in using a well-known word to remember something new. For instance, my name is Anne and I am learning the routine for answering telephone calls at my new office, I remember A for 'answer', N for 'number', N for 'name' and E for 'extension'.

Reducing the amount of information to be remembered

Earlier we mentioned that one of the essential qualities of internal strategies is that they reduce the amount of information we have to get into our storage files. There are many ways of doing this—for instance grouping and acronyms.

Grouping   This involves grouping or 'chunking' bits of information together. Many of us do this when we put new phone numbers into storage. We might split the phone number into two parts. Association can also be used to add further meaning. The following example makes use of the date of Australian Federation—the year 1901.

A friend moved into a new home a few years ago, and of course had a new phone number. He described it simply as 534-federation, a little easier than 534-1901!   Scott

To remember a long number, such as 256983, you could split it into two, and remember it as 'two hundred and fifty-six and nine hundred and eighty-three', or you might prefer to use the rhythm 'two-five-six, nine-eight-three'.

Some people remember a list of things to buy at the shops, by grouping similar items together. Then they can use the categories of

* The colours of the rainbow: Red, Orange, Yellow, Green. Blue, Indigo, Violet.

items to help remember each item . For example, if you wanted to buy the following items:

bananas	yoghurt	milk
cheese	pears	oranges
honey	cake	sugar

and you were not able to write down a list to take with you, then it might help if you group the items into categories. How would you group these items? When you get to the supermarket, you then have to recall the categories, and what was in each of them. 'What **fruit** do I need to buy?—of course, it was bananas, oranges, and pears. And what about the **dairy produce**—ha yes, cheese, milk and yoghurt. Now the last thing, **sweet foods**, what were they—um—sugar, cake, and honey.'

Acronyms   Acronyms are another way of reducing the amount of information to be remembered. You take the first letter of each word in a list and use these initial letters to make up a new word.

Many of you will be familiar with 'ROY G BIV' as a way to remember the colours of the rainbow in order. All you have to do is run through each letter, and recall what each letter stands for—Red, Orange, Yellow, Green, Blue, Indigo, Violet.

One person advised us that an associate had been chairman of the Swan Hill Irrigation Trust, but never used the acronym!

Maybe this prompts you to think of some acronyms that you have found useful.

Mnemonics

The word 'mnemonic' comes to us from Greek mythology. The Goddess of memory was called Mnemosyne, and her nine daughters were the Muses.

Books or training courses for 'improving your memory' often describe mnemonic (pronounced nee-mon-ick, with the stress on 'mon') techniques—some are quite complex. We have found these more elaborate techniques difficult to apply in everyday situations. Here are a few examples to test out.

'Method of Loci' This mnemonic strategy uses visual association of objects with a predetermined set of locations. Let's say that you want to impress your friends by remembering a list of ten shopping items in a particular order. To do this you could imagine walking through your house, and visually associate the ten items on the list with ten locations in your house.

So you might associate the first item, let's say it is **milk**, with the **front door**. You could imagine opening the front door to collect the milk after it has been delivered. The second item might be **bread**, and you might imagine the bread on your **hall table**. You then continue to imagine walking through your house, associating each item with particular locations, in the order that you would see these locations as you walk through your house. When you need to recall the list of items, you take a mental trip through your house. You imagine each item sitting in its location and reel off the list. Wow—how clever!

This technique is fine for lists of words. But it is not very often that many of us need to remember a list of words in a particular order. We have tried the technique with more everyday remembering, such as lists of names of people and wines, but found these more difficult to visualise, which made the technique even more complex.

Peg-word method Another mnemonic technique to test out is another seeing 'in your mind's eye' or visualisation method, called the peg-word method. The idea here is to visually associate the objects on your list of 10 words with another list of words, which are remembered using a rhyme.

You will first need to learn the following rhyme:

1 is a bun

2 is a shoe

3 is a tree

4 is a door

5 is a hive

6 is sticks

7 is heaven

8 is a gate

9 is a vine

10 is a hen

You can see that each number is associated with a word that can be transformed into a mental picture or image. For this technique, you will associate the first word from the list, that is 'milk', with a bun. You might visualise a bun going soggy because it has milk spilt all over it. You continue on. The second word 'bread' is associated with 'shoe'. What image could you create to link these two? When you want to recall the list, you recite each line of the rhyme one by one, and remember the vivid image that you have created to link the two objects.

Some people use these elaborate internal techniques, which they have practised and perfected, to learn amazing amounts of information. Unfortunately, being able to remember 100 digits after only hearing them once, or learning a list of ten phone numbers in ten minutes does not mean that you will be able to remember where you put your wallet, when to turn the sprinkler off, or that the saucepan may boil dry if not checked!

These strategies can be useful when we are studying for exams or learning a complicated set of procedures for a new technology—for example, computer programming—but they do not improve your memory overall, and are generally used to recall things that most of us do not commonly need to remember in our everyday routine. Moreover, they are not user-friendly and can require a great deal of effort and time for success. You also have to 'remember' the details of how to apply the strategy, and if you are experiencing difficulty with getting new information into storage, this could be a problem. When you have to remember a list of ten items to buy at the supermarket wouldn't it be much easier to write them down, and take the list with you?

 ## External memory strategies

As we discussed earlier, memory strategies can also make use of external aids.

These external strategies work best when we are organised. Someone with a good memory is usually a well organised person, but it is also true that a well-organised person has more chance of remembering well. It is often at times when we are disorganised that we begin to wonder about our memory abilities—when we are busy, rushed, stressed, in unfamiliar places, on holiday, moving house or without assistance at work.

Being organised helps to get the most out of all the memory strategies that we have discussed. For example, you might keep very good notes in your diary but forget to look at it at the right time, or even worse, forget to take it with you when you need it. Or you might have written a detailed shopping list, but not be able to find it anywhere.

The strategies or devices that become part of your daily habits and routine will be the most beneficial. They will reduce the demand on your memory. If you use a diary, for example, it helps to make checking your diary something that you do at the start of every day— part of your routine in the morning, or the last thing that you do that day. You can keep your shopping list in a designated place—for example, attached to the fridge in your kitchen. If you have special places for things, make sure that you put them back in that place when you've finished with them!

If you are really into routine, you could even try to do things at set times of the day, or on set days of the week. For instance the rubbish has to be put out on Mondays, the pot-plants need watering on Tuesdays, and your weekly luxury massage is on Thursdays. This helps to take the load off memory even more.

It's a good idea to **act immediately** whenever possible. When you think 'I must water that plant', and it is possible at the time—water it right then; then there's no need to remember it later. Similarly, use your memory aids as soon as possible—if you are cooking and use the last of the sugar—write down on your shopping list **at the time** that you need sugar next time you do the shopping. Or if you are lying in bed at night and think 'I must remember to put my film in to be developed tomorrow', write this down on tomorrow's date in your diary, or on a piece of paper that you keep by the bed, or get up and put the film by the front door. Many people forget these sleepy inspirations by morning.

I am so busy at the moment it's ridiculous. I find that if I don't write something down at the time that I think about it—I completely forget about it later. My diary is my life-line! I don't know what I'd do without it.   Russell

I'm always leaving things behind or forgetting to take something I intend to. What I do now is to put the items ready—when I think of it. I might put a book in the car when I know I have to return it to the library the next day, or put letters that I have to post on the hall floor. **Mandy**

Many people use external strategies as a 'back-up' system for their memory. The very process of putting the back-up system into action makes us focus attention on the thing to be remembered, so we often don't have to use the system—but it is reassuring to know that it is there. For example, the process of writing something down on a calendar might make it easier to recall that information later on and we might not have to refer to the calendar at all. Writing out a shopping list helps us in remembering what we wanted to buy—this is especially useful when we get to the shop and find we have left the list at home. And don't we feel proud of our achievement when we get home and check the list to find we got everything!

Common external strategies involve writing things down, putting something in a special place, alarms and technical devices, and asking someone to remind you.

Writing things down

There aren't many of us who haven't written something down so that we will remember it later. We don't really need to say very much about this particular external memory strategy. It is probably the most common. However, there are many variations on this theme and you may find that there are some that you haven't tried before.

People use written memory aids for remembering just about anything!

Where something is located   We often use written memory aids to remember where things are. We label folders, so that we know what is in them. We label drawers of filing cabinets for the same reason. Sometimes it would be very useful to have a few more labels around the home!

Some people write down the level that their car is parked on, when it is in a multi-storey car park. You can write it on your ticket if you take it with you, in your diary or perhaps resort to the back of your hand!

For that odd occasion when you do leave something behind, some suggest that you write or engrave your name and address for return on things that you might leave around, such as your umbrella, book, spectacles or handbag.

Something that you have to do   People use diaries or calendars to help them to remember social events, appointments, medication for pets, and other important things to do.

Memory is the diary that we all carry about with us.   Oscar Wilde, 1895

Calendars are often used as 'social planners'. If something is written on the household calendar, then everyone in the house knows about it, and this can avoid double booking. It is important to hang the calendar in a place where everyone will see it and to look at it regularly. Next to the phone, on the fridge or in the kitchen are all good locations.

My husband is always up-to-date on our social plans now—I've hung the calendar in the toilet!   **Philippa**

A diary is useful if you are often on the move—you can take it with you wherever you go. It helps to get into the habit of checking your diary as part of your daily routine. A diary that allows space for a list of things to do is doubly useful.

Whiteboards or blackboards in strategic places are sometimes preferred to pieces of paper that tend to get lost. You can write on the back of your hand, even with lipstick, or on the mirror if desperate! Leaving your notes in attention-grabbing places can often jog your memory about something that has to be done. Sticky 'Post-it' notes must have been designed for exactly this purpose. Their bright colour makes them stand out—but beware, they have been known to fall off!

I put a post-it note around my front door key to remind me to do something when I get home.   Judith

What to take with you   When you are about to go on holiday you are usually very busy, tying up all those loose ends before you go. It can be very helpful to write down not only what you have to get done but also what you have to take with you. If you tick off each item on the list as you pack it, and take a final look at the list before you leave home, then you are more likely to remember everything you need.

We have a holiday list for the family which we keep in a special drawer and pull out each time we go away.   Jackie

What to buy   We all have different ways of compiling a shopping list, and it is something that most of us do regularly. Some people hang a list in their kitchen, and write things on it as they discover they need them. Others compile a list just before they go shopping. Some people have a pre-printed list of commonly needed items, and tick each one as needed. Others are even more organised...

I have a very analytical mind and like to list my weekly grocery shopping in the same order as the rows of the supermarket. This saves me time and having to retrace my steps, to go back to aisle 5 to get the olives, etc. The system worked well until a decision was made to enlarge and remodel the

store. It quite threw me out and I didn't know whether I was Arthur or
Martha for several weeks.   **Terry**

What people tell you   One of the most common times that we have to
remember what people tell us, is when we take a **phone message**. For
this, it is useful to have a pad by the phone. It is even more useful to
have a pen there too—one that works—preferably attached to the pad.

Many people carry a **notebook** with them at all times. This can be
useful for jotting down things that people tell you, that you will want
to remember later—good books, nice wines, names of plants that you
admire, new phone numbers and addresses—the list goes on! Some
people find it helpful to take notes when they visit the doctor. It can
be useful to prepare what you want to talk about, and also to note
any particular suggestions that the doctor outlines. It is also handy to
keep a note pad in the car.

If you attend lectures or seminars, it can help to remember what
was said if you take some notes. You will need to keep track of where
you keep the notes and it helps to summarise key points later to
internalise the memories—or tell someone about it.

Address books and **birthday books** are another example of
written memory aids. Not many of us are able to remember all our
friends and colleagues' names, addresses, phone numbers, fax numbers and birthdays without looking them up.

Names   Written memory strategies can be very useful when it comes
to remembering people's names. At social gatherings, people often
use **written name tags** for this purpose. Receptionists and doctors
often have name plaques on their desks. Name tags work best if they
are in large print, so that people can readily read the first name.

I work in marketing, and I think it's important to address people by their names. I have a pad by the phone. When someone says who they are, I immediately write down their name. Then I can say goodbye, using their name. It also gives me a handy record of whom I have spoken to during the day.   **Paula**

Record-keeping   When you think about it, written memory strategies play a big part in our memory of things past, in literature and history.

On a personal level, we write things down in diaries (for that future autobiography!), photo albums (written captions), travel diaries and 'baby milestones' books. We may want to retain the details of a recipe we created, or that one a friend tells us, or that one we heard over the radio. A kitchen 'record book' is a good idea for this (or use your car 'day book' if you are a car radio listener!). Written records of past financial accounts are often consulted. Some people keep written records of presents they have given people, and lists of people they send Christmas cards to each year.

I've done it twice now—given the same present to my mother and my brother two years in a row. It was such a good idea, that I thought of it again! Mum loves sunhats, and Hugh loves books about gardening. Needless to say, I now keep a book in which I laboriously list the presents that I give to people each year.   **Catherine**

For work, we keep a written curriculum vitae or a resume, and at our jobs we often record daily statistics. Remembering to use the travel log book in the car for recording kilometres driven is essential for income-tax claims for some working people.

Putting something in a special place

Where something is located   Some people have set places in their home or workplace for specific things that they use, especially **things that they use regularly**. Wouldn't it be great to always know where your keys, your wallet or purse and your glasses are?

When you first work out the special place to store objects, it can be helpful if you think of it, and where you have put it, **at regular intervals** afterwards. If you make these intervals a little longer each time it can help reinforce your memory of where something is stored.

Another idea is to store the object in a **function-related spot**. For example, many people store their keys near the front door of their house. This makes sense, because most of us pick up our keys as we leave the house, and it is easy to put them back there when we return.

What better place to keep your spectacles than around your neck? Attaching a chain or band to your glasses that allows you to hang them around your neck means you always know where they are. Apparently this particular memory aid is a trendy one too!

I was always losing my ticket in car parks. Then I discovered that the visor on the windscreen had a little strap on it. Now I always know where my car park ticket is, because as soon as I get it, I put it under the strap on my car visor.   John

This brings up an important point. When you've finished with something, make sure that you **return it to its special location**, ready for the next time that you are wondering where it is.

Something that you have to do   If you put something in a special place, where it is **visible**, then it will act as a reminder to do something. You are more likely to act on that reminder if you see it. How many times have you heard someone say 'out of sight, out of mind'? For example, if you put a letter to be posted by the front door, or with your house keys, then the next time that you leave the house you will see it and be more likely to post it.

If you need to remember to **take certain medications**, you can put them near the thing that acts as your memory trigger. For instance, if you take your tablets after you brush your teeth, put them near the toothpaste. If you take them with meals, put them somewhere obvious in the kitchen.

I was at my parents' house for dinner. The news was on TV and I was watching a story about a house fire, where two children had died. I suddenly remembered that I had forgotten to turn off my perfumed oil burner candle that was sitting on my desk, surrounded by papers. I panicked and I could feel my heart thumping in my chest. 'Oh no—our house could be in flames, and it's all my fault.' My fear was exacerbated by my recollection of another news story about a house fire caused by someone leaving their oil burner on. I rang our neighbour—who, thankfully, informed me that the house was still standing when she had driven past it five minutes previously. Since then I've put the oil burner by the study door. Now I can't help but see it—and of course blow the candle out—before I leave the room!   **Sophie**

Some people find it useful to have a reminder that's in view most of the time, or that they can't avoid seeing. We have heard of many different ways to do this, including putting a ring on a different finger, putting a knot in your handkerchief, putting a rubber band on your wrist, and putting your watch on the opposite wrist. You may have other ideas.

One of the best hints that I have read was in a women's magazine. Whenever you put your car lights on, lock your door. To get out of the car you will have to unlock your door, and this will remind you to turn off your lights.   **Trish**

What to take with you   Some people have a special place for things that they need to take with them each day, like the hall table near their front door. Others create an obstacle at the front door with the object that they need to take with them so they can't forget it! The front door is also a useful place to put a 'sticky note' telling you what to remember to take with you, or what to turn off before you leave.

Another option is to put what you want to take with you straight into your bag or brief case. It helps to do this as soon as you think of it.

At work, I often used to leave my food shopping in the fridge, instead of taking it home at the end of the day. Someone gave me a great tip. If you put your car keys in the fridge with the food, you can't leave work without it! I use this idea to remember lots of things—I just put my car keys with whatever I need to remember to collect.   **Malcolm**

It can be very frustrating when you leave your bag or umbrella somewhere, especially on public transport. One idea is to put these items in front of you, where you will trip over them as you get up to leave.

Where you are up to in a book   A special place that we often put something into is a book that we are reading. A bookmark can be made of exquisite embossed leather, or be a simple scrap of paper. Or you might be lucky enough to have one attached to the book. Having it attached to the book has the added advantage that you don't have to spend time looking for the bookmark. Bibles, prayer books and old classics used to always have a silken thread as a book-mark.

Alarms and technical devices

Something that you have to do   A common example of this is when you use the timer on the oven to remind you to take something out when it is cooked. The **oven timer** is actually a very handy household reminder. You can set it to remind you to do many things—to turn the sprinkler off, to take the hand-washing out of the basin, or to wash the dye out of your hair. You just have to make sure you can **hear** the timer. There are also inexpensive portable timers available. For some household devices you can buy specific timers. For instance, timers can be attached to water taps and lights to turn them on and off. Many people use these timers on their light switches, radio and tape-recorded dog barks for security in their homes when they go away on holidays.

If you want to get more technical, you can use all kinds of **electronic gadgetry** to remind you of something that you need to do— from the simple watch alarm to the more complicated personal organisers.

A man who was experiencing memory problems came to see me. He arrived a little early for his appointment. After we had been talking for a few minutes, I heard an electronic beeping noise. The man looked at his watch, and told me that it said 'Appointment with Anne Unkenstein at 2.30 pm.' He was one step ahead of his watch!   **Anne**

A special device that can be useful when it comes to remembering to take **medication** is called a 'dosette box'. This is a plastic box, divided up like a grid, into the days of the week, with different time slots. You can sort your various tablets into this box, which serves as a reminder to take the tablets and also keeps track of the last time that you took them. Many people use home-made variations on this theme.

Where something is located   Electronic devices are very handy when you want to find something. Some people find their keys with key rings that whistle back when they whistle.

Locating your car in a carpark can sometimes be made easier if you have a beeping remote-control locking mechanism that you can set into action.

Cordless phones are wonderful inventions, but very difficult to find at times. Fortunately, most have a handy button to press on the part that is plugged in, which makes the handset tell you where it is by beeping repeatedly until you pick it up.

Ask someone to remind you

People are often excellent external memory aids (or aides)! You can always ask someone to remind you. If a person is not available, you can get machines or telephones to do the work. Organise a telephone reminder call to wake you up or leave a message to yourself on your answering machine to remind yourself to do something.

Other people also make willing external memory aides when it comes to recalling names. Don't be embarrassed to ask—many people experience difficulty with remembering from time to time. At a social gathering or meeting, you can quietly ask someone the name of a person that you are about to talk to, before you walk over to them. Alternatively, if you meet someone and you recognise their face but can't recall their name, it's OK to say, 'I recognise your face, but I can't recall your name at the moment.' You can sometimes even manage to have a conversation with someone without having to address them by their name.

I'm good at remembering faces, but not names. My wife is good at remembering names, but not faces. So whenever one of us has trouble recalling a name or a face, we just ask each other for help. We make a good pair!   Barry

When we go to social gatherings, my husband helps with my poor memory for names. For example, if we walked up to a man called Greg, he would include the name Greg at the start of our conversation, so that I could hear it. 'Hello, Greg, we haven't seen you for a while...'   Beth

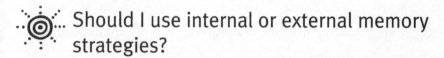 Should I use internal or external memory strategies?

People sometimes think that it is 'lazy' to rely heavily on external strategies, and may be concerned that it will make their memory worse: that they need to 'use it or lose it'. This is not the case.

The brain isn't like a muscle. External memory aids aren't like crutches that allow muscle wastage. Conversely, you may become very proficient at using one or more of the internal techniques, but this will not make your memory better, in general. With extensive training and practice you may develop the extraordinary power to remember a shopping list of 135 items, but this doesn't mean that you will be any better at finding your car keys, and if you can't drive to the supermarket then your memory of the 135 shopping items will not be required! However, for some people who have not consciously used mnemonic strategies, it may be fun to try one out!

Similarly, repeating the same thing over and over in order to get it into your memory files may help you to remember what you have been repeating, but it will not make your general memory abilities better.

'To reject memory aids when they could make life easier is like rejecting reading glasses when you need them...don't feel ashamed...what matters is that you continue to deal effectively with the environment.'[9]

External memory strategies are often easier to use

Most people, especially older people, tend to favour external strategies over internal. They are easier to use; they can also be great fun
and involve a bit of creativity, whereas the more complex internal
strategies are not so 'user-friendly', requiring a great deal of training
and practice to master. Research shows that people tend to stop using
internal strategies after a while. For instance, four months after a
group of people had been trained to use the 'peg word' method, half
the people used it 'very little', and the other half did not use it at all.[10]
Some memory researchers even make the confession that they do not
use their techniques when they leave the lab!

External strategies suit everyday memory better

Everyday memory typically involves remembering things that we
have seen or heard only once, or remembering to do something. For
this type of daily memory use, external strategies have been found to
be more suitable. Researchers have found that external rather than
internal strategies are better for remembering to do something.[11]

External back-up systems create time for creating!

We have an increasing amount of information to remember in these
complex times. Sometimes it is just not practical to try to remember
all of this information using internal strategies alone. It makes good
sense then to have back-up systems, that we can refer to should the
need arise.

Using external strategies as back-up systems for remembering the
more mundane aspects of life also leaves the mind more available for
fun and creative pursuits. It means that you can turn your often limited attention elsewhere, and perhaps discover new things. For

example, you can fill your diary up with names and appointments, and in your memory filing cabinet reserve your energy and time for organising the storage of more exciting information. This way, you will be able to more efficiently sort through when you want to recall information.

Albert Einstein is often quoted as an example of this. Apparently he said that he wouldn't waste his mental energy on learning his home phone number. He had other, more exciting ideas that he wanted to occupy his mind with.

 ## Using the strategies that suit you best

I interviewed a 73-year-old man at the kitchen table in his derelict house hundreds of kilometres from Melbourne. The first time I asked him when a particular event occurred, he stopped, then silently rose to a standing position and walked to the outside door; he stood there, peered outside and returned to his seat and answered '1956'. About two minutes later I asked another question, about his family. Again he rose, walked outside, went to the doorway and peered out and when he returned sat down and proudly said '8th May 1961'. It just didn't make sense—so I said, 'What takes you to the door?' He answered—with a glint in his eyes—'All my important dates are painted on my outside water tank and the one way to remember them is to get up and look.'   Julie

When it comes down to it, the best memory strategies for you, as an individual, are the ones that you prefer, and the ones that best suit your own unique situation. You will probably use a mixture of internal and external strategies that suit you and your lifestyle.

The strategies that you use now will also depend on what strategies you have used for memory management in the past. We tend to stick to what we are familiar with. You may also notice that your need for and use of strategies fluctuates over time. When we are busy, and our workload is heavy, it can be useful to rely more on external strategies, which use less of our available mental energy.

I used to try to keep all my 'to do' plans in my head, but now things have changed. I'm a lot busier—in a managerial role at work. I'm now in my mid-thirties, and I can't rely on 'my head' to remind me, because if I forget something important at work I'm in trouble! I've noticed that I have begun to write 'to do' lists on scraps of paper, which I carry around everywhere with me. The only problem with this is that sometimes I can't find the piece of paper. The other day I left it in a meeting, and when I eventually remembered where I had left it, and went back to collect it, someone told me that they had thrown it out.   **Tony**

Tony obviously finds that having a written memory back-up system gives him peace of mind. To make it work even better for him, he might find it useful to write his 'to do' lists in his appointment diary at work, and get into the habit of checking the list regularly. This way he will avoid losing the list, and always remember to look at it because it has become part of his daily routine.

As you have been reading about the many different memory strategies, you most likely have found some that are very familiar, some new ones which appeal to you and others that you could never imagine using. You may also use some which have not been mentioned. Tell someone about these and check if they also use some strategies which are not described here. Talking about memory strategies reinforces the fact that they are as important as any other area of our own self-care, and this will contribute in turn to us developing more 'memory-friendly' communities.

The power of long-established sensory 'cues' can be used deliberately as part of memory strategies; you 'pull up' memories using particular sensory associations. Everyone learns from a very early age to associate certain memories with smell, tastes, sounds, sights and touch and movement; but certain people seem to be especially good at a particular type of sense memory (which can be developed and used professionally, as in the case of wine judges or chefs). Sometimes people will have become habitual in the way they use certain combinations of these senses to 'get information in'—e.g., they'll remember spoken information by taking written notes and using a particular coloured pen, or looking at the speaker and writing or telling someone the essential points very soon afterwards. Everyone is different and we all have our own preferences for memory strategies. For example, some people find that visual strategies suit them best, whilst others find that they need to write things down in words if they are to be any use later.

Whenever Sue gives me directions, I have a lot of difficulty following them. She likes to describe the route we are to travel in words, telling me about certain features along the way, that I will see as I drive past. I much prefer a picture to guide me—an actual map I can see, and then visualise in my memory as I drive.   Helen

The type of strategy that you use will also depend on your lifestyle and personal interests. What do you need to remember? Are you trying to find your wallet? Are you trying to recall someone's name? Where are you at the time? Are you driving a car, and not able to write something down? You will probably have found that you need to use a different strategy for each situation.

No one can tell you which memory strategies will work best for you as an individual. Managing your memory is a dynamic and individual process and may change substantially over your lifetime. Our general guidelines may be helpful, but even these can only be applied to the extent that they suit your lifestyle. **Strategies need to suit you so that you will actually use them**.

You will probably find that you have a range of specific strategies for specific situations that you encounter. It may be useful to review your current needs and decide whether you need to 'polish up' the strategies that suit you as an individual or develop new ones. Be creative! Many people find that it is easier to create new memory strategies which are based on ones that they already use than to change their methods. Some people have always used a message pad by the phone, others like to have a 'things to do' pad, while others prefer a running notebook. Again, it is fun to share your strategies in discussion with others.

What is important is that you are aware that there are strategies you can draw on to get the most out of your memory.

Key points

• Check influencing factors that can cause fluctuation in remembering abilities, and take action as required. See the checklist on page 64.

• Use memory-friendly strategies:
  a) internal ones, those which involve mental management; and
  b) external ones, using memory aids as a back-up system.

• Strategies need to suit you as an individual—choose the ones that best suit you at this stage of your life.

• As life circumstances change, there may be benefits in testing out new strategies.

• Discussion with others about memory-friendly strategies they find useful can be very illuminating.

6

Changes in **someone else's** memory: what can we do?

As our society becomes more tuned in to memory problems and the possibility of dementing conditions, we begin to worry about other people's memory as well as our own. The most frequent response that young adults made to us when we told them that we were writing this book was 'When can I get it? I need to read it for me—and I will give it to my mother!'. In this section we will address common fears held about our Nearest and Dearest—be they family or friends.

The concerns people have are usually threefold.

- What is happening to my Nearest and Dearest? Do the changes he or she is showing indicate early signs of dementia or other permanent memory losses?

- If so, what are the indications for me as I get older?
- How am I going to handle these changes in my Nearest and Dearest?

In previous chapters we have outlined the normal changes that happen to memory as people get older. Chapter 3 outlines many factors that can adversely influence memory from time to time. When you have concern about someone else's remembering abilities, take the time to think about these factors and their potential influence on this Nearest and Dearest person of yours.

⊙ Is anything making him or her more forgetful than usual?

Check out this summary list.

- Does your Nearest and Dearest expect her memory not to be working as well?
- Is any medication being used? Is this likely to affect her memory?
- Is his alcohol intake more than usual?
- Has her vision been impaired in any way?
- Is his hearing becoming a problem?
- Is chronic pain present?
- Could hormone levels be fluctuating?
- Do you think that being depressed or 'down in the dumps' might be an issue?
- Has there been a high level of anxiety or stress?
- Is the workload too heavy?
- Is the level of mental stimulation adequate?
- Is he or she eating, exercising and sleeping well?

One or more of these factors may be affecting memory at the moment. In addition, not paying attention to things is often related to not being able to remember them later. Some people declare that they are making a lot of 'memory mistakes', yet it may well be that in fact they lack interest or motivation to learn particular things.

Helping out with some memory strategies

When memory strategies are being discussed with a Nearest and Dearest it is extremely important that this person is not patronised, 'put down' or made to feel embarrassed.

We all use memory strategies in our own ways throughout our lives: they are not just 'dreamed up' to fix problems in old age! And they are used to maintain our basic identity and not as a 'copout' from 'really using my memory'.

Sharing our personal strategies and showing how we value them is often an important way to help a Nearest and Dearest to acknowledge new options for better memory management.

The way that you go about this will depend on the circumstances.

Being direct

If the Nearest and Dearest talks to you about being forgetful, then you in turn can openly discuss memory strategies with him or her. This can be very helpful to you both. The strategies section in the previous chapter of this book may provide you both with some ideas to test out, or you can share some of your strategies, and invite your Nearest and Dearest to do likewise. You might even be able to laugh together about some of your successes and failures!

Remember that some inefficiency in memory is normal when any of the factors in the checklist above are at work. Talking about your strategies for remembering provides a good opportunity to think of new ways that such factors can be better controlled or even eliminated.

Being less direct

For some people—and there are lots of reasons why—questioning or raising the issue of their memory abilities is not on! In this case, you will need to find a respectful, subtle approach that respects this person's dignity. Ideally, this will lead on to discussing the problem directly, which will in the long run be a much more effective approach:

It's amazing how frequently I find that there is a history of the adult children discussing their concerns about their Nearest and Dearest's less effective remembering long before they raise the issue, upfront, with that person. This is usually the stage when family seek professional advice.   **Anne**

The approach you use will be strongly influenced by the nature of your existing relationship and the demands on your Nearest and Dearest's memory abilities. You need to find out what are the typical things that he or she tends to forget, and work out some strategies which will suit those specific situations and be useable for that person. The demand on people's memory becomes much heavier when they are in unfamiliar situations.

My brother took Mum away on a family holiday. He found it was easy to overload her with too much information at once. When they arrived at the house he took her on a quick tour, telling her where everything was, including the light switch. The next morning, she declared that she hadn't slept well because she couldn't find the light switch in her room. The next night he let her know exactly where the switch was just before she went to bed—providing limited information, and at the time and place when it was needed—and there was a much more successful outcome.   **Tina**

In another family, the mother was often confused about which night she would go to each adult child's house for dinner. The family didn't want to talk directly to her about this because they thought she would take offence. In the end they worked out a really good way to get around the problem. They worked out a weekly routine, so that dinner at each particular house was on a particular day of the week: Tuesday night was Suzie's house, and Thursday night was Nick's house. This lessened the demand on the mother's memory, and achieved the desired result in a subtle and respectful way.

Another anecdote concerns a daughter who wanted to indirectly remind her father about things he often forgot, such as appointments and remembering to bring certain things with him. She found it helpful to telephone him and say things such as 'I am looking forward to our lunch at twelve o'clock today,' or 'I want to check if I did ask you to bring...'—a tactful way to give a reminder, and safeguard the quality of the relationship.

The following stories illustrate some common situations. For each story we will comment on the memory difficulties described, and suggest strategies that may be useful for better memory management. Clearly you may think of other strategies which would have suited you better had you been in the situation.

'My mother's memory is getting worse and she and my father fight all the time now...'

My elderly mother and her second husband seem to be fighting and angry with each other whenever I visit now, calling each other names like 'senile', 'stupid', 'useless', and Mum complains about Brian whenever we talk on the phone. But I find that she is the more forgetful of the two, and it is worrying me. She even forgets what she has been saying mid-sentence sometimes, and gets really cranky with any of us if we tell her we have heard it all before. She seems to be blaming Brian for her own memory lapses—as if he were at fault and the cause of them. I think she is getting worse—how can I help? Is she getting Alzheimer's Disease? I'm really worried.   **Judy**

Let's draw out the essentials of the situation.

Judy's mother

- is forgetting many recent things;
- doesn't want to acknowledge her memory problem and is blaming her husband;
- doesn't want to talk about it.

Judy, meanwhile,

- is worried about their relationship;
- thinks her mother is developing dementia;
- wonders how to handle this;
- and asks 'What does it mean for me?'.

What might Judy do?

We suggest she uses an indirect approach, that she seeks information about normal change in memory with ageing, and finds out about Alzheimer's Disease by contacting the Alzheimer's Association.

Addressing her mother's fear of change, expressed as anger and blaming of her husband, may be the first indirect step in this case. Judy will not help by telling her mother she 'shouldn't blame and name-call'. She can help her mother best by listening and then, when the outrage has subsided, telling her mother how she, Judy, worries when she hears the anxiety and anger in her mother's voice on those occasions. There will be many strategies which family and friends can choose from to manage conflict, and one of the most successful things is to avoid telling people what they should/ought to/must do or not do, and instead speak in first person as what 'I' would like, want, fear, think, feel about...

In respect of Judy's anxiety about her mother's apparent denial and about what may happen with her mother's memory 'down the track', more subtle strategies will need to be called on. Talking with a counsellor at the Alzheimer's Association or at a memory clinic could be helpful to Judy. Such a discussion could also deal with Judy's concern about herself. Finding out about memory change with age and with disease from this or other books would be valuable as well.

'My father is so proud about his wartime memories, but...'

My father doesn't want anyone to know he has problems with his memory— he is 83 and he has terrific memory for the war and his old friends and work colleagues, but he can't remember the smallest things he may be told—even messages from his friends at the bowling club he doesn't seem to recall, and he has missed lunch engagements and meetings at the club which he agreed to and wanted to attend. I'm worried about his pride getting in the

way of his continued social life—he seems to think its something shameful
to have memory problems at his age!   Jenny

We see that Jenny's father

- has difficulty with recent memories;
- is ashamed, and will not publicly acknowledge memory shortfalls;
- is at risk of increasing social isolation.

We see that Jenny

- is worried about her father's social life;
- doesn't know how to help him deal with his pride.

What might Jenny do?

- She might reinforce his pleasure in his memories—she could encourage him to write down some of his wartime stories.
- Her initial approach would be indirect: She could talk with some of his wartime friends and colleagues about how they manage their own memory, and ask have they noticed her father's need for some memory assistance. She could request that someone regularly collect him for club meetings, and give him written club messages and appointment details as reminders.
- She could use a direct approach: she could say that she has read this book, talked with other people of his age and discovered it is normal part of ageing to experience this type of memory change and it is not a shameful thing.
- She could invite him to look with her at the use of some of the external strategies in Chapter 5 and try out some which appeal to him.
- If she's decided to go for the direct approach, she could also give him a whiteboard and a diary for his next birthday.

'My mum's old neighbour wanders in at all hours...'

An old neighbour of my 75-year-old mother has taken to visiting her much more frequently and at unusual times. She seems to want to talk, but is a bit vague about what day it is, what time it is and has even asked when my father is coming home (he has been dead for over 10 years!). My mother likes Betty and they have been good supportive neighbours over many years. Her family doesn't visit much, since they all live interstate. I'm worried about my mother who has a serious heart condition and chronic rheumatoid arthritis, taking on the responsibility of caring for Betty. I've tried to persuade her to write to Betty's daughter, but she doesn't like to interfere, as Betty says she doesn't talk to her children any more. I don't know that this is true, given Betty's memory failings. I'm concerned that Betty needs some place to live where she can be with company and under some supervision to prevent her injuring herself, and not putting a load on my mum! **Anna**

Anna's problems are that she
- assumes that Betty is a burden on her mum;
- is anxious about her mother being physically at risk due to responsibility of caring for and Betty;
- is anxious to have Betty cared for by someone else but doesn't know how to arrange it.
  What might Anna do?
- The first question she needs to ask is whose problem is it? So she needs to be direct in asking her mother whether she finds Betty's visits too much for her or whether she enjoys Betty's visits.
- She needs to know if Betty visits other neighbours.

- She could usefully contact a carers' association such as Carers Australia or Age Concern (UK) (see page 128) for guidance in how to assist a neighbour who appears to be socially isolated and with memory problems.

 ## Seeking advice, assessment or treatment

If you think that it is necessary, encourage your Nearest and Dearest to seek advice or treatment for the factors that you believe may be adversely affecting his or her memory at the moment.

If you are concerned that your Nearest and Dearest may have the beginnings of dementia, read through the section about dementia and Alzheimer's Disease (Chapter 4). A memory assessment may be the next step.

Key points

- Check if any outside factors are influencing the person's memory in an adverse way.

- If you think it is necessary, encourage the person to seek advice or treatment for these factors.

- Help out with some memory strategies. You may be able to openly discuss memory strategies—or you might need to be more subtle with your assistance.

- If you are concerned about Alzheimer's Disease, read the section about dementia (Chapter 4). You may want to suggest memory assessment.

7

Towards a memory-friendly community

We are living in a constantly changing society. There is an ever-increasing amount of information available to us now. Life is busier, the pace is faster. There is more to do and see—and remember.

Our physical environment changes. New freeways are built, which means we have to learn new routes to travel. New shopping centres are built, or old ones are modernised. The shop that you went to last week has moved, or the supermarket has rearranged its aisles.

We now move from one work environment to another more often. Many older people move from their homes into alternative accommodation facilities. All this moving means there is more to learn, in a never-ending process of making the unfamiliar familiar.

We are constantly having new technology thrust upon us. Computers, electronic banking, new telephone systems, mobile phones, fax machines, CD players, microwaves, video machines and video cameras. There are new ways that information about how to use prescribed drugs is given to us by the chemist, or by the doctor. There are all sorts of new aids to help people with disabilities, and new names for community and health services and the municipalities in which we live.

Multiple changes such as these place an unprecedented demand on memory capacity. Because of this, continuing education is in high demand, and has become a major focus of many workplaces. At work and at home, we are constantly finding we need to keep 'up to date', but there never seems to be enough time. Not so long ago, people were able to consider that by early adulthood they had attained most of what they needed to know about their field of expertise. These days, it seems that knowing everything is impossible.

On the other hand, there is so much information that no one is expected or required to remember all of it. In fact, in some places of work, people may be actively discouraged from trying to gain information other than that which is absolutely essential for their prescribed tasks at a given time—it is more important that they be able to re-train quickly when the demands of the job change. It is clear that the old patterns of steady acquisition of skills have given way to patterns based on flexible learning and efficient use of memory. Ideally, our society should be responsive and proactive in enabling people to learn how to adapt to this new situation—especially less advantaged middle-aged and older people who may otherwise be 'left behind'.

More people experiencing changes in their memory abilities

In addition to these social changes making more demands on the memory abilities of all members of industrialised, technically driven societies, there is a demographic shift: the proportion of older people in our community is increasing. This means there are more people experiencing real change in their memory abilities as a part of normal ageing.

As a community, we need to be aware of the quite considerable individual variation in memory ability. We need to accept that there is change in memory abilities around us, and ideally, achieve a culture which makes allowances and provides support for this from time to time— a memory-friendly (and therefore age-friendly) community.

As an example of how we can do this, consider the perennial problem of remembering people's names. Perhaps we shouldn't expect another person to remember our name. Maybe a new social etiquette would suggest that we say our names when we meet people. This has the added advantage of encouraging them to spontaneously say their names too!

Wouldn't it be great if we could feel comfortable, rather than embarrassed, when asking someone to tell us their name? For example, 'I remember you very well, but your name has slipped my mind for the moment.'

'Putting on face'—the fear of forgetting!

I was going to lunch in the city with some work colleagues one day, and we were at an intersection. A comparable group of businessmen was about to cross, coming towards us from the opposite side. One of my friends, who is a very gregarious chap, near retirement age, saw an 'acquaintance' in the other group, and vice versa. Initially, they raised eyebrows at one another, and as the lights changed and they walked towards one another they began to smile broadly. In the middle of the road they shook hands vigorously and exchanged greetings.

'Good to see you again, how's it going?' asked my friend.

'Terrific. And how have you been?' he replied.

As they talked on and explored when and where it was that they last met, they eventually concluded, in the protective confines of the midstreet tram shelter, that they had never met before and didn't know each other from a bar of soap.   Terry

 ## Talk about memory!

With more to remember in our daily lives, and more people in our community experiencing real memory change, it's surprising that many people do not openly discuss memory. Almost the only way of approaching the topic that is sanctioned in Western society is through therapy—for example, psychoanalysis, hypnosis, regression or rebirthing, reminiscence therapy and post-traumatic stress debriefing. Less sensational, although just as intriguing and important to our lives, are the workings of day-to-day memory, but these are rarely talked about.

A communal fear of memory loss seems to make it a 'taboo' subject. Yet if there were more discussion about the fluctuations that a lot of us experience in our remembering, then the fear and anxiety surrounding memory loss would lessen. People would realise that it is quite normal to experience memory change, especially as we get older, and that one small memory lapse doesn't mean you are developing dementia. People would be reassured that they are not 'the only ones' to experience fluctuations in their memory abilities.

Many people get themselves into a downward spiral. They become anxious because of a memory lapse. Then, because they are so aware of their remembering abilities, they notice every memory lapse that they make, no matter how small. They become more anxious, and often don't tell anyone about their fear. The increasing anxiety means that they are more likely to 'forget', as a result of poor attention. They then notice more memory lapses and, in turn, become more anxious.

If only we could feel more comfortable talking to others about our concerns, then we might break this cycle. If we stopped covering up our lapses, then we would also stop putting unnecessary expectations on ourselves. We would realise that they are most likely normal fluctuations, and by talking to others, we might pick up some new ways to manage mild memory changes.

The other day Mum, who is 61, told me how she keeps forgetting where she puts things. I said, 'How about finding out about some ways to help your memory?'. She immediately changed the subject, and somewhat angrily moved the cups into the sink! I could tell that she really didn't want to talk about it.

A few days later, she told me that her forgetting was making her panic, and she often wondered if she was going 'senile'. When I had suggested that she do something about it, I think it made her panic even further, as if it confirmed that I thought she was losing her memory too. I think I had reinforced a lack of trust and confidence she had in herself.   Eva

If Eva's mum had known a little more about what can happen to memory as we get older, then she might not have panicked about becoming 'senile'. If she had felt more comfortable in talking about her fears and knew that they were normal for her age, then she might have been able to come up with some useful ways to manage the slight changes she had noticed and her sense of panic might well have diminished. However, people who are afraid about losing their memory are very quick to pick up suggestions which may reinforce their fears. This easily leads to denial and rejection of any help that is offered.

If we talk more about memory strategies, then people will feel less embarrassed about using them. They will know that many other people rely on them too.

How to make our community 'memory-friendly'

As a community we can lessen the demand on everyday remembering by making alterations to our environment and our socially accepted skills of communicating.

Most of us cannot keep all the information that we need in our lives 'in our heads'. What we need are better ways to access information when it is required. We need a 'memory-friendly society'. We need changes in our homes, workplaces and community as a whole that will reduce the amount of information that we need to keep 'in our heads'.

There are many 'memory-friendly' examples around us already, but we can always do better! We can make more clever use of signs. Where? Almost everywhere! Inside buildings—shopping centres, large department stores, hospitals, large office blocks; outside buildings—at schools, universities, accommodation facilities, holiday units, public transport centres, car parks; on nature walks and tourist routes; consistent use of symbols and signage for names of streets, children's crossings and to warn drivers of various features on the road (speedhumps, winding road)—signs to tell you where the toilets are and 'staff only' or '—'s room' signs.

Signs can take many forms. They can be written, or pictorial. Pictorial or symbolic signs are very powerful and are usually culturally universal. Location maps are increasingly popular, with 'You are here' clearly marked on them.

We can design places to make them 'memory-friendly'. It is easy to get lost in new environments. If we use special design features, we can make this less likely.

Making each part of a large place unique in some way will help you to remember your way around it. If it all looks the same, it's easy to get lost!

Some places are using coloured lines on the floor to direct you around them. We've seen this in hospitals, in large car parks and in aircraft. Car parks could also include colour coding to tell you what level you're on, and perhaps pictures, as well as numbers. Remembering that you are on the level with kangaroos painted all over it may come to you more easily than remembering that you are on the third level!

I drove my car into an underground car park of a major hotel. I had a companion with me and we were to attend a politically sensitive, very important meeting. The park had many circular 'offshoots' and I clearly did not pay enough attention to where I left the car. On my return I became footsore as I searched level after level and odd corner after odd corner—and still no car! I went back to reception, ordered a taxi, and finally located my car in an area I must have passed and re-passed. I'm sure many a reader would be quick to tell me what I should have done—and their own awful experiences!

Car-park strategies—what I have learned:

- to recognise the power of distractors;
- to acknowledge the influence of stress on paying attention;
- to give myself time to safeguard identifying cues which will be useful later;
- to carefully record (write down if necessary) the identifying sign or number for the location of my car;
- to give myself a long-stemmed carnation as a bonus for successfully recalling the location of my car!   **Delys**

Special accommodation facilities or nursing homes, that often cater to people with a degree of memory loss, can also be made more 'memory-friendly' by the use of appropriate signs, colours, furniture difference, noise, lighting etc.

Design of household or work-related objects can also be altered to make them place less demand on memory. Objects could even be marketed according to how 'memory-friendly' they are. We could have a five-star rating system for 'memory friendliness'!

Instruction booklets are a must with any new devices. They should set out the steps clearly, and be able to be displayed somewhere where the user can refer to them again and again. Written and pictorial instructions can be combined to reinforce memory.

Instructions that are permanently displayed on objects are invaluable, especially for objects such as photocopying machines and fax machines that people may not use often, and which require constant refresher courses for proper use! These also tend to have unique instructions for each individual machine, which makes it difficult to manage replacement equipment.

Phones are becoming more memory-friendly, with design elements like memory buttons for frequently dialled numbers. This is useful for people who find it difficult to recall phone numbers, unless you have a two-year-old visitor who presses the long-distance numbers that you have carefully programmed! Cordless telephones often have electronic devices that allow you to trace them.

You can now buy cameras that include date stamping, so you don't have to remember when you took the photo, just where!

New car designs are including more and more 'memory-friendly' features. In some cars you can't lock the doors if the lights are on. In others you can only lock the door from the outside, so you never lock your keys in the car. Many cars have lights or special alarms that come on to remind you that you need more petrol or oil, or that you have your lights on when you stop the engine.

Medication is being packaged in ways that reduce the load on memory. Some packets have scratch-off tabs for each time that you take a tablet. All you have to do is remember to scratch off the tab! Other medication packets are arranged like a calendar, to help keep track of your daily intake.

Many workplaces now display a photo board of staff. This includes a photo of each staff member with the name underneath it. This can be handy for clients and fellow staff alike. How about a photo board of your key tradespeople, your neighbours?

◉ Create time for creating

We are not suggesting that everyone should sit back and stop using their memories. What we are suggesting is that 'memory-friendly' back-up systems in our environment will free people's minds for other, more creative or interesting pursuits.

If, for example, it takes you less time to find your car in a car park because you remember where it is more easily with the help of the kangaroos, then you will have more time to use your memory for other things—remembering what the after-dinner speaker said, for example—and you are less likely to have an accident when you drive out of the car park!

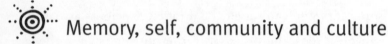 ## Memory, self, community and culture

A strong sense of self can be protected and enhanced through memory 'care'. For 'generation MM', that is, people who will spend the majority of their lives in the years 2000, memory 'enablers' will no doubt be high on the agenda. Current cohorts of older people will be advantaged by their (younger) Nearest and Dearests encouraging an acknowledgement of the need to adapt to the normality of age-related memory changes, by incorporating remembering strategies into their lifestyles. Conversely, if we assume that memory 'loss' is an inevitable part of ageing, we will not value our own old selves. Moreover, anxiety about memory incompetencies and supposed impending dementing conditions, together with an almost universal fear of ageing, morbidity and death, will prevent our memories working well, prevent us being positive agers.

Positive ageing has become a community issue in many societies, as evidenced in political interest shown through parliamentary enquiries, provision of access to learning for older people and the development of special community facilities for retirees in sport, the arts and travel. To make use of these opportunities, the individual relies on having good recall for rules, procedures, timetables, who owns which possessions and where they belong—and even telephone numbers and your own names! Otherwise, an infrastructure is required to provide assistance and care, and participation is restricted.

Just as memory supports the individual self, community memory sustains the selfhood of a society. Mature societies value their histories, their records, their literature as part of cultural identity. Where languages (and memories) are lost through disuse, or through one culture taking over another, histories are lost also, for the dominant culture records only what it thinks is important or credible.

Let's make remembering well part of our individual and community thinking, and in so doing seek to enhance the dignity and self-respect of every citizen, young and old.

References

1   Ackerman, Diane, *A Natural History of the Senses*, Phoenix, London, 1996

2   Kral, V.A., 'Senescent forgetfulness: Benign and malignant', *Journal of the Canadian Medical Association*, 86 (1962), pp. 257–60; Crook, T., Bartus, R.T., Ferris, S.H. *et al.*, 'Age Associated Memory Impairment: Proposed diagnostic criteria and measures of clinical change—Report of a National Institute of Mental Health work group', *Developmental Neuropsychology*, 2 (1986), pp. 261–76; Caine, E.D., Nomenclature and diagnosis of cognitive disorders: a US perspective, Abstract from Age-related Cognitive Disorders conference. Nice (Glaxo), June 1992; American Psychiatric Association, *Diagnostic and statistical manual of mental disorders: DSM-IV*, 4th edn, American Psychiatric Association, Washington, DC, 1994

3   Rose, S., Internet article, 'No way to treat the mind', 1996. Steven Rose is Head of the Brain and Behaviour Research Group at the Open University.

4   Dawson, D., and Reid, K., 'Fatigue, alcohol and performance impairment', *Nature*, 388 (1997), p. 235

5   Newens, A.J., Forster, D.P., Kay, D.W.K., Kirkup, W., Bates, D. and Edwardson, J., 'Clinically diagnosed presenile dementia of the Alzheimer's type in the Northern Health Region: Ascertainment, prevalence, incidence and survival', *Psychological Medicine*, 23 (1993), pp. 631–44

6   Jorm, A.F. and Henderson, A.S., *The Problem of Dementia in Australia*, 3rd edn, Australian Government Publishing Service, Canberra, 1993

7   Jorm and Henderson, *The Problem of Dementia.*

8   Rose, Steven, ABC 'Health Report' transcript, Internet, March 1997

9   Singer, George and Lirl, *Making the most of your memory—Practical memory exercises for all ages*, La Trobe University Press, Bundoora, Victoria, Australia, 1994

10 Kotler and Camp, in Lovelace, Eugene, *Aging and Cognition: mental processes, self-awareness, and interventions*, North Holland, Elsevier Science Publications, Amsterdam & New York, 1990

11 Kotler and Camp, *Aging and Cognition*.

12 Ackerman, *A Natural History of the Senses*.

Several of the quotations used in the text are drawn from *The Penguin International Thesaurus of Quotations*, compiled by Rhoda Thomas Tripp, Penguin Books, Harmondsworth, 1976

What to read and where to go

The following books are suggested for those who might want to read more about how memory works and how to deal with memory changes. Also listed are organisations concerned with ageing and dementia; details for these bodies were correct at time of going to press.

How memory works

Most books on this topic are academic textbooks which are not aimed at the general reader—they tend to be heavy going. The following are exceptions.

Baddeley, A., *Your Memory: A User's Guide*, Penguin, Harmondsworth, 1983

Schachter, D.L., *Searching for Memory—the Brain, The Mind and the Past*, Basic Books, New York, 1996

The effects of ageing, and dementia & Alzheimer's Disease

Biggs, Simon, *Understanding Ageing—Images, Attitudes and Professional Practice*, Open University Press, Buckingham, 1994

Birren, J.E., and Schaie, K.W., *Handbook of the psychology of ageing*, 4th edn, Academic Press, California, 1996

Most Alzheimer's Associations hold excellent reference library resources which we would encourage you to visit. We recommend:

Hoffman, S.B. and Platt, C., *Comforting the Confused: strategies for managing dementia*, Springer, New York, 1991

Jorm, Anthony, *Understanding Senile Dementia*, Chapman & Hall, Melbourne, 1991

Mace, Nancy, *The 36-Hour Day: a family guide to caring for people with Alzheimer's Disease*, revised edition, John Hopkins University Press, Baltimore, 1991

Sherman, Barbara, *Dementia with Dignity: A Handbook for Carers*, revised edition, McGraw-Hill, Sydney, 1994

The Alzheimer's Association in Australia can be contacted for the cost of a local call on 1800 639 331. Or phone them in your state or territory on:

ACT (06) 238 1288	SA (08) 8372 2100
NSW (02) 9805 0100	Tas (03) 6234 8884
NT (08) 8941 3963	Vic (03) 9818 3022
Qld (07) 3857 4043	WA (09) 388 2800

The Carers' Association in your state or territory can be contacted on:

ACT 1800 817 746	SA 1800 815 549
NSW 1800 817 023	Tas 1800 818 776
NT 1800 817 901	Vic 1800 814 215
Qld 1800 017 223	WA 1800 816 040

Readers in the UK could try

- Age Concern England, Astral House, 1268 London Road, London SW16 4ER, tel. (0181) 679 8000, URL http://www.ace.org.uk/links/default.htm (this Website lists many bodies in Europe and North America that focus on ageing and Alzheimer's)

- Alzheimer's Disease Society UK, Gordon House, 10 Greencoat Place, London SW1P 1PH, tel. (0171) 306 0606, fax (0171) 036 0808, URL http://www.vois.org.uk/alzheimers

New Zealand readers can contact

- Alzheimers Society, PO Box 2808, Christchurch, tel. (03) 365 1590, fax (03) 379 8744

- Age Concern New Zealand Inc., PO Box 10–688, Wellington, New Zealand, tel. (04) 471 2709, fax (04) 473 2504

- Mental Health Foundation, PO Box 10 051, Auckland, tel. (09) 630 8573, fax (09) 630 7190

- Senior Citizen Unit, Social Policy Agency, PO Box 21, Wellington, tel. (04) 471 0321, (04) 472 4543

In the US, try

- Alzheimer's Association, suite 1000, 919 North Michigan Avenue, Chicago, Illinois 60611 1676 tel. 312 335 8700, fax 312 335 1110.

- American Association of Retired Persons, 601 East Street, Washington DC 20049, tel. (202) 434 2277

- National Institute on Aging, PO Box 8057, Gathersburg, MD 20898–8057, tel. 1800 222 2225

- National Mental Health Associations, 1021 Prince Street, Alexandria, VA 22314–2971

- All areas of the US have an Office/Area Agency/ Commission on Aging. There are also various state agencies.

Memory strategies

Most of the books available focus on 'memory improvement' using complex mnemonic techniques. If you would like to have a go at some of these strategies, the following books describe them:

Crabtree-Morton, J., *Improve Your Memory*, Penguin, Harmondsworth, 1996

Singer, George and Singer, Lisl, *Making the most of your memory—Practical memory exercises for all ages*, La Trobe University Press, Bundoora, Victoria, Australia, 1994

Other books of general interest

Ackerman, D., *A natural history of the senses*, Phoenix, London, 1996

Schama, Simon, *Landscape and Memory*, Fontana Press, London, 1996

Index